THE STREETS
WHERE
WE LIVED

by
David Young

First published 2000 by David Young
The Shieling
19 Orchard Grove
West Winch
King's Lynn, Norfolk

A catalogue record for this book is
available from the British Library.
ISBN 0-9539686-0-X

Chapter I

HALT! WHO GOES THERE?

IN Stockton Road, Durham City, roughly opposite the gates of St Oswald's cemetery, was a well-trodden path which ran through the centre of an extensive area of allotment gardens. My father called the area Klondike, a reference perhaps to the original "gold rush" for these invaluable flower and vegetable plots when they were first created. The allotments were bounded on the east by the foot of Mount Joy Hill and a track that runs alongside it up to the farm. On the west side there was a stream which ran down from Little High Wood, a useful source of water for the gardeners. On reaching the verge of Stockton Road, near the Science College caretaker's house, the flow disappeared into a culvert, no doubt eventually to form one of the streams that ran into the River Wear from its steep banks near St Oswald's church.

The path from Stockton Road through the allotments brought the walker to a small embankment which climbed to another path leading into the wood – a popular place of exercise and recreation for the neighbourhood. It was where families took the air – and perhaps collected firewood – and was a scene of many childhood adventures.

Dad and I had left our Highwood Terrace home one day in late 1939, or maybe early 1940, taking our pet fox terrier Rex for his customary walk. We had crossed the road to Klondike and were half way along the track when we were stopped – but this was not just for the sort of chit-chat that such encounters usually involved. "Identity card," demanded a man sporting an official arm band. Dad: "Haven't got them. We're just out for a short walk through the wood."

"Sorry, I need to see your identity cards, Harry," insisted the officious one.

"But you know who I am," Dad protested, clearly irritated that one of his lifetime acquaintances should be so unreasonably obstructive.

"Identity cards." The voice was sterner now, reinforced by the authority an ARP armband invested in its wearer.

We turned for home. Even as a small child I sensed that something about the world had changed and I didn't have to wait long to find the reason.

"Don't you know there's a war on," yelled the officious one as we trudged off disgruntled.

* * *

I spent my formative years during the war and just after in Highwood Terrace and Hallgarth Street (the epicentre of our branch of Durham's then extensive Young family). It was for the most part, though not entirely for me, a happy time. Now that I've retired and lived away from Durham for 40 years I still feel an affinity with the streets, the school, the church and the people who were my mates all that time ago. I will be touching on aspects of family and community life and how ordinary working people once dwelt in the terraces and villas that now appear to be so much dominated by university folk and clogged with cars. A very different world indeed but at the same time still very familiar.

Shortly after I left Durham in 1960, I wrote a letter to the *Advertiser*, high in indignation but weak on fact, I guess, protesting at the demolition of a small estate of council houses, called Hatfield View, to make way for university development. My theme, if I remember it rightly, was that the university should push off to Brasside or Framwelgate Moor to expand its campus and leave the nicer parts of the city to its true inheritors, the local people. How naive.

I was severely chastened by a knowledgeable respondent in the following week's *Advertiser* so, living as I did 200 miles away, I gently retreated from the debate. I was embarrassingly reminded of this rash intervention by a lady of 90-plus who told me on a recent visit: "Hatfield View was a miserable place to live. The houses weren't any good. They suffered a lot of damp with the mist rising from the river and most people couldn't wait to get out."

Enough said on that particular episode. But, as in most communities, there is a great affection for the past in Elvet and St Oswald's parish and a lingering regret among remaining locals at some of the changes that have taken place – particularly the increased student population in a tight-knit area and an imbalance of property occupancy brought about both by university expansion and by the increased mobility of families, such as my own, that has been a feature of late twentieth-century life. This work is not a serious social history, however, merely a personal indulgence – reminiscences and fragments set against my family background that I hope may be enjoyed by past and present inhabitants of Durham's ancient Elvet ward.

"Names sell papers" was an early lesson I learned as a cub reporter on the *Durham Advertiser* – so I will weave as many as I can remember into my narrative, hoping to be forgiven for any faulty recollections.

* * *

27 Lowes Barn Bank was where I was born in October, 1935. It was then the last house on the left before the bank began to descend more steeply towards Stone Bridge on the Neville's Cross to Langley Moor road. I recall little about the house, other than it compared favourably with my subsequent childhood homes, because it had the mod. cons of the period: a modern cooking range, hot water, bathroom and so on, with a decent sized garden at the rear.

It was a garden with a good view over the countryside and Dad used to lift me up to point out the Silver Link as it raced along the main railway line in the distance.

I have a vague recollection of some special event occurring when I lived there – a visit by some notable personage,

BELOW: Doesn't he look sweet? Mam shows me off to the world with pet fox terrier Rex in the garden of 27 Lowes Barn Bank.

perhaps a Royal, whose motorcade passed down the bank as residents turned out to watch. (This may have been a visit to Durham by King George VI and Queen Elizabeth in 1939 but why they were on this particular route I do not know.)

And I remember being walked along to Langley Moor to a barber's shop for that ritual hated by little boys, the first haircut. I'm pretty sure I howled and I certainly was not impressed when the barber tried to humour me by describing the electric shears as an aeroplane. Mam shopped at Wait's, a modern shop on the corner of Potter's Bank opposite the Duke of Wellington inn. A special treat was a trip into Durham on the little red town service bus that set off from there.

Lowes Barn and nearby Merry Oaks were an up-and-coming suburb of the city which by then had also sprawled out on to its other moors of Crossgate, Gilesgate and Framwelgate. The attraction of Lowes Barn for my parents, who married in 1933, might have been its convenience for my father's workplace, Fowler and Armstrong's garage and coachpainting works situated on the upper reaches of Potter's Bank, almost opposite the Chief Constable's house.

What was behind their decision to move, I have never known, nor will I now. I suppose I was never curious enough to ask. Perhaps they were feeling the pinch. It was, after all, Depression days and I don't suppose Dad was ever highly paid. Perhaps it was the onset of the war, or the feeling that life would be more convenient nearer the town, or that they were thinking about my schooling. The most likely explanation was that money was needed for the dreaded doctor's bills after my mother had been diagnosed with the TB that was soon to claim her life.

Whatever the reason, the move to Highwood Terrace, in purely property terms, was a step down. The previous occupant of No. 6, the end house, had been a well-known Durham character and musician called Tom Gascoigne, who played the organ at the Regal cinema in North Road (later the Essoldo).

The amenities were basic: a scullery with a cold water tap and sink; an old-fashioned black-leaded kitchen range; and a toilet and coal house in the backyard, in which hung the galvanised zinc bath. Soon we moved along to No. 4 which had been vacated by a Mrs Manuel and which I guess, was slightly larger. The Wards (Fred, Lizzie, née Walker, and her sister) moved into No. 6 and lived there for many years. All this change was a bit of a puzzle for a four-year-old but the houses seemed cosy and it was certainly a happy and pleasant area in which to live – and appears to have remained so to this day.

For a start, there was a social life. There were children. I cannot recall having any playmates, nor indeed having contact with other kids at Lowes Barn Bank. But in the back lane of Highwood Terrace and in Highwood View there always seemed to be an abundance of children out playing. Many became pals for ten years or more, well into teenage at the end of which National Service, first jobs and other new horizons brought a natural parting of the ways.

It didn't take me long to make a lasting impression on new playmate Paul Allison. His home at 3 Union Place shared the same back lane and I was taken along by Mam to meet him. When the introductory formalities were complete, Paul's Mam produced a wooden hammer and peg board, a commonplace toy of the day.

Regrettably, I'd never seen the like before and having possibly been reared thus far on only soft toys, I found it strange. When handed the hammer, I promptly smote young Paul a smart blow on the head. A split second's silence and look of shock quickly crumpled into tears and loud wailing. A severely embarrassed and apologetic mother hauled me off for a good hiding (not uncommon in most households in those days). But the rift was soon healed and Paul became a regular playmate, and I was a frequent visitor to both his house and Mrs Smith's, his grandmother's, at No. 1 Highwood Terrace to play games on wet days.

No. 3 Union Place (near to the former Union Foundry) was set back from the frontage of Highwood Terrace and, though not a very large house, was better equipped, notably with indoor toilet and bathroom and, curiously, with a servants' bell system (by then defunct), the indicator board remaining as a relic of an earlier lifestyle in the living room.

Paul's dad, Ernie, was a white-collar worker, who studied hard, and became chief financial officer of Easington Rural District Council. He was also well-known as a Cathedral bell-ringer and later there were occasional fascinating Sunday afternoon visits to the belfry. Paul had a younger sister, June, and later there was Susan, a post-war baby – common in many already established families.

Going out to play for the first time can provide a child with an insight into some of life's harsher realities. For a start not everyone is going to be as nice as you expect. For me, taking a new trike out on its maiden voyage in Highwood View was an experience in which eager anticipation was quickly transformed into tearful dismay. I was a stranger to the other children and a subject of curiosity in my own right. And my trike? Wow, that was something they all wanted to ride, though there were others in the street. So on its first outing I was relegated to a somewhat crestfallen spectator. I was soon accepted, however, and became with experience what is now called streetwise – though occasionally falling victim to my own innocence.

My very early upbringing would be best described as sheltered. I cannot ever remember really bad language ever being used by my parents, for example. "Damn," "heck," "blithering," "blinking" and "blooming" and maybe one or two more substitutes for stronger expletives seemed to be the limit of my father's vocabulary of oaths. Whether his language was more colourful at work or at the pub I don't know but I imagine it was.

So I went out into the wider world of communal play with innocent ears and a receptive mind. The first offending word I picked up – not immediately realising its significance – was "bugger."

It appears even more ugly printed than said. But forgive me, because asterisks will lessen the impact of the anecdote, the point of which is the explosive effect this awful outburst from her only child had on my rather gentle mother. I suppose I entered the house repeating this fascinating word I had picked up in the street.

"Bugger." Mam immediately flew off the handle and went for me, catching me with a clip round the ear and pursuing me round the living room. "Bugger," I repeated. She was angry and distraught. Under the dining table I fled. "Bugger, bugger, bugger." Mam's failing energy was not up to dealing with the situation and things calmed down. I kept muttering the word quietly and repetitively, hypnotised by the response it had provoked.

Until Dad came home, that is. The pleasure of my daylong defiance was exceeded only by the painful lesson inflicted. No hiding place under the table this time.

* * *

Highwood View was a relatively safe place to play, away from the main roads and with very few resident vehicles. They included Hindmarch's yellow coal lorry and Arthur Almond's handcart from which he conducted his flourishing plumbing business. Hedley's brought milk from Farewell Hall on a horse-drawn cart and it was measured out from a churn into your jug. Later came milk by the pint and half-pint bottles from Mount Joy Farm with the familiar cardboard caps that the blue tits used to peck off, given the chance. These tops, from which a centre piece could be removed, were often collected and bound with raffia to make table mats and similar items, as part of the wartime make-do-and-mend attitude I suppose.

Crampton's, the greengrocers from Elvet Bank, came round with their horse and cart as did Eddie Thew, also from Elvet, though it was not until later that he had a shop. Fish was sold from flat carts, leaving a watery trail from the melting ice in the fish boxes. "Calla herring" was a familiar cry.

Street theatre for kids was provided by the knife-grinder whose elaborate cart-like contraption sent sparks flying as he treadled the belt-driven grinding wheel to sharpen housewives' knives and scissors. And on foot came the rag and bone man Paddy. A fearsome figure to little ones because parents would threaten: "We'll give you to Paddy if you're naughty." In scruffy garb – usually an old gaberdine raincoat – he would shuffle round the streets, sack over his shoulder, yelling: "Rags, bones", "Jam jars."

If children were about he'd make to chase them and they'd scuttle off giggling and laughing, not knowing whether to be afraid or not. He never actually seemed to collect anything but I suppose he must have done. And as we grew older and bolder, of course, the tables were turned. We baited him – but in a less playful way than he had baited us. Rather cruel really.

Chapter II

PUT THAT LIGHT OUT . . .

Shortly after we moved to Highwood Terrace, the war made itself apparent. Even as children we had a vague sense of something unusual going on. There was talk of it it "all being over by Christmas" but clearly Christmas came and went without it all being over and the effects of the conflict, though still distant, became more tangible. Our encounter with an ARP warden which I have already described was an illustration of the phony nature of the war's early days and this sort of local officiousness faded as the war went on.

At the outset, underground shelters had been dug behind the Science College on the edge of the field at the foot of Little High Wood. I was certainly carried there two or three times by my mother after the siren had sounded in the middle of the night to join the rest of the local community in this cold and inhospitable refuge. As far as I can remember, there was none of the cheerful camaraderie and bonhomie that was reputed to have sustained the Cockneys in their shelters during the Blitz. We just sat there frightened and miserable until the "all clear" sounded and the danger was deemed to be over.

In fact, the danger proved to be virtually non-existent and any time spent in the dank, dismal, cold and smelly shelters was so awful that they rapidly fell into disuse, families preferring to retreat no farther than the cupboard under the stairs or under the dining table to defy Hitler's worst.

Later in the war people simply stayed in bed listening to the distant sounds of bombs and guns banging away in the Tyne, Wear and Tees industrial areas and being aware through the closed curtains of searchlights trawling the skies to trap the raiders. There would be a frisson of fear,

RIGHT: Dad with NFS colleagues at Elvet Waterside, near Baths Bridge, where the authorities had requisitioned part of McIntyre's garage for war use. Father (left, front) joined the fire service at the start of the war and served until well after 1945, mainly at stations on Tyneside, Felling and Walker included. On release he had a variety of jobs, including van roundsman from our shop at 17 Hallgarth Street, before settling in a civilian post at the county police garages at Aycliffe, the then HQ.

though, when the bomb blast was a little nearer, rattling the window panes perhaps, and sending heads quickly under the bedclothes. The house was duly decked with blackout curtains, according to wartime regulations, and windows were criss-crossed with brown paper sticky tape lest they shatter in a bomb blast, scattering lethal shards. ARP wardens patrolled and were quick to let any residents know if as much as a chink of light escaped. "Put that light out," the voice yelled.

But the most dramatic development as far as the Young household was concerned was my father leaving work at Fowler and Armstrong and becoming a member of the Auxiliary Fire Service (AFS), which, as the Home Front became better organised, was renamed the National Fire Service (NFS). To this day I can remember dad's service number, because it rhymes, as being 004470 – double O, double four, seven O.

Dad was not a tall man – about five foot eight – nor was he heavily built. Though his working clothes were overalls and sometimes a little shabby, he liked to dress up in his best togs and when he did so was quite dapper, his favourite rig being sports jacket and flannels with highly-polished brown shoes. Throughout my childhood, the breast pocket of his jacket would sport a blue silk handkerchief, a gift from mother. If he wore headgear,

it would be a tweed cap or a trilby, an item of apparel few well-dressed men were seen without in the Forties.

So, when he arrived home one day in his new black uniform, with peaked cap, shiny buttons and badges and a very heavy webbing belt complete with axe, he looked very impressive to my young eyes.

Of course, many dads donned a uniform and went off to the war and were away for long periods, and I've often since wondered whether dad's was a "compassionate posting" on account of my mam's failing health. Or, having been born in 1903, was he too old? The fire station was at The Sands and, for me, seeing the pumps and fire engines even in their wartime grey rather than shiny red, was a little boy's dream. The whole experience was somewhat less romantic for dad and the first inconvenience we experienced as a family was his shift pattern of 48 hours on, 24 off.

The war brought a somewhat depressing effect to the street scene – buses and official vehicles "camouflaged" to a drab grey-green instead of their usual bright colours. At night street lamps remained unlit, car and motorbike headlamps were cowled to an extent that they were almost useless. To help the hapless driver, kerbs, trees and other prominent obstacles that his vehicle might come into contact with were painted with bands of white. All direction signs and place names and anything else that might prove useful to a stranger were removed to confuse the expected invaders.

Brick-built air raid shelters with re-inforced concrete roofs were rushed up – three, each to accommodate 50 people, were sited in what had been St Oswald's School's garden in 1939 – and square tanks of bolted sheet steel appeared at strategic points. Bearing such words as "EWS – 5,000 gallons," these were to contain emergency water supplies for use by firefighters – by the end of the war they also contained much rubbish. Some of the school's classrooms were taken over by the ARP for a while and St Oswald's Institute was commandeered by the army for the duration.

On a personal level, people had to be aware of various drills and regulations and, for a while, carrying gasmasks in their strong cardboard boxes with a cord shoulder or neck strap was an inconvenient must. These were terrifying appliances for children to wear and even a "Mickey Mouse" version failed to calm the fright of the little ones.

Apart from one well-documented incident, the city appeared not to be high on the Luftwaffe's priorities so the men in the fire service were despatched to areas where their services were more urgently required and my father told me in later life of travelling to Hull on an open fire engine to reinforce the hard-pressed local crews in an area that was heavily bombed. I could never imagine him being involved in anything dramatic but he told me once – and once only – that he and a trailer pump he was working were blown into a dock by a bomb blast. How he survived he never said. But I know he couldn't swim. As for Durham, local mythology had it that the Cathedral had been singled out for attack in the series of what became known as Baedeker raids which devastated Coventry. It was a bright moonlit night but as the bombers approached a mist rose up from the river safely concealing the target.

This was regarded as a miracle and there were plenty of "witnesses" ready to testify to it. Indeed the story was first recounted to me by my stepmother Florrie (née Butterfield, formerly of Boyd Street and Church Street Head) who had been a fire-watcher and though not on duty herself that night was well acquainted with those who were. It's a nice story, of course, but the question remains: if Durham were such an important target why didn't the Germans come back another night?

A plausible theory was that the Cathedral's majestic towers, set over the distinctive loop in the river, were so prominent a landmark that Luftwaffe crews, having just crossed the coastline, used them as an invaluable navigation aid and were unlikely to destroy them.

An excellent account of this historic event that so excited city residents at the time appears in Martin Dufferwiel's *Durham – a thousand years of history and legend*.

* * *

My natural mother had been born in High Street, Norton-on-Tees, near Stockton, in 1904. The youngest of four – she had two brothers and a sister, all of whom lived out their lives on Teesside – Sarah Jane Suddick (known as Jenny) grew up in that picturesque village, complete with tree-lined High Street and duckpond, and was baptised, confirmed and married at St Mary's Church. One of my keepsakes is a small Bible with the price of 4/6 pencilled in the flyleaf and the inscription in ink: "Presented to Jenny Suddick by her brother William on her 11th birthday, November 1915." Beneath has been added: "Presented to David by his Dad, December 1, '48." How many brothers would buy their sister a Bible as a birthday gift today? How indeed would it be received?

It was always a treat to visit my grandma who by then lived in Fox's Almshouses farther down High Street, the family home at No. 25 having been demolished and redeveloped as shops. Norton's near neighbour was the vast ICI complex at Billingham and the sight of barrage balloons in the sky protecting it from attack is one of my earliest wartime memories.

It is not entirely unknown for a journalist's personal communications to be a bit lax and over the years I have regrettably lost touch with the Suddicks of Norton. The aforementioned William, Uncle Billy, who worked for the ICI, and Auntie Hilda, brought up quite a brood at 12 Milner Road – Raymond, who went to sea; Marjorie, Joan, twins Lesley and June (around my age) and Valerie. Lesley, the one I knew best, occasionally visited us in Hallgarth Street with a friend in her teen years to look round the Cathedral or Castle, to take a boat on the river and to have tea with us. She ultimately married a clergyman and went to South Africa. Uncle Harry, a gardener when I was a child, and Auntie Molly lived in Station Road, Norton, and brought up my cousins Ena and Vera, sadly now no more than names from a distant past. Mam's sister Auntie Mary Crawford had married a widower and lived at Dormanstown, near Redcar. Her stepson was killed on active service with the Fleet Air Arm during the war. Cousin Marjorie and her husband turned up to represent the clan at Dad's funeral in 1972.

When I was small visits to grandma's were always a treat, not only for the bus journey, but also for the excitement of meeting cousins. My earliest memories of her are dominated by domesticity – dough rising on the hearth in the process of breadmaking giving off a delicious aroma; the dressing of a crab, always something of a ritual with grandma knowing the secret of which poisonous bits to discard; bringing delicious curd cheesecakes from a baker's in High Street opposite the almshouses. But her sight soon began to fail, possibly through cataracts, and later she invariably wore an eyeshade. I well remember that her pouring tea became a hazardous experience and you had to be ready to leap out of the way lest you were scalded. Her small home contained a treadle sewing machine, a picture of Queen Alexandra that seemed to dominate the room and horsehair dining chairs that prickled my legs when I was still in short trousers. I was rebuked for fidgeting. Another significant item was her radio set provided by the Royal National Institute for the Blind with braille markings on the knobs and switches to help her tune in. My cousins and I played in the back yard and back lane and my memories, though somewhat faded, are sunny ones.

I believe my mother was grandma's favourite child and she was very distressed about her TB. When grandma herself was on her death bed years later I made the journey from Hallgarth Street to Norton by bus to see her. I was about 14 and went alone. Auntie Mary took me into the bedroom to see her, warning me that she might not recognise me. Grandma was clearly in her last throes, in pain, in delirium, perhaps from the effects of morphine, and trying to sit up, unable to see. It was so sad and ironic – and a little frightening. "Here's David come to see you," Auntie Mary announced. But in her desperate final agonies grandma, reaching out, cried: "Is it Jenny? Is it Jenny?" I was led away.

How proud I was, though, several days later to sit next to the chauffeur in the big Daimler that accompanied grandma on her final journey from the Fox Almshouses to St Mary's Church for the funeral. Later Auntie Mary came to Durham and brought me £20, I think, from grandma's estate. The end of an era. The only grandparent I knew.

* * *

How my mother met my father, or indeed ended up in Durham, I do not know. But she worked in Boots the Chemist in Silver Street, giving up her job on marriage, or shortly after, as was the custom at the time. Our family album includes a picture of a large group, including my father and mother in evening dress, at a function in the Masonic Hall, Old Elvet, in 1931. Dad was not a freemason, far from it, so my assumption is that it was Boots' staff party. Despite having photographs, I have always found it difficult in my mind's eye to hold onto a clear vision of my

BELOW: This picture was taken by the Durham photographers Fillinghams in the Masonic Hall, Old Elvet, on January 28, 1931. My father is in the third row from the front, just right of the centre of the picture with his bow tie looking somewhat askew. In front of him is my mother, wearing a corsage, then his bride-to-be Jenny Suddick, of Norton-on-Tees. Was this an annual party for staff of Boots the Chemist, of Silver Street?

mother – other than that perhaps she was near my father's height, slim, and from an off-spring's viewpoint good looking. People talked about her being good at needlework and to this day we possess a tablecloth colourfully embroidered with flowers.

Even in the late Thirties, Mam did not have long to live. How long did it take her illness to manifest itself? Was she or my father aware of her fate by the time I was born? In any event, I was shielded as much as possible from the unpleasant situation.

Life in Highwood Terrace was at first normal. I started St Oswald's School, I went out to play. We walked the dog. Dad went to work. Mam cooked the meals, did

BELOW Courting days. Pictures taken at a Middlesbrough studio, D. A. Maclean, in the early Thirties. Dad has signed his picture "Love, from Harry" and Mam, a more formal "Miss J. Suddick, with love."

RIGHT: Mother and unknown friend. Her bridesmaid when my parents were married at Norton-on-Tees was Miss E. Gatenby. Perhaps it's her.

the housework, went shopping and occasionally played the piano. Soon, however, tuberculosis took its toll. Mam spent longer in bed upstairs. It was not long before she was totally bedridden and brought downstairs into No. 4's front room – an ominous move but not recognised as such by a puzzled child. The effects of TB are

distressing with the patient coughing up blood while wasting away and suffering feverish night sweats. I was kept out of the way as much as possible but I believe the end came when grandma from Norton was staying and her shouts to rouse my dad, who was in bed, disturbed me. "Harry, Harry, it's Jenny!" I'm not sure whether I actually recall this or not. But it's how it seems.

St Oswald's parish register shows that she was buried on October 30, 1941, aged 37, shortly after my sixth birthday – her death on October 27 from pulmonary tuberculosis having been certified by Dr R. Caile MB and registered by my father the same day. She lies in the Stockton Road cemetery, near the wall that bounds School Lane.

Of course, losing one's parent was not so uncommon at that time and I noticed in the extract from the parish register that shortly after my mother's burial followed that of James Forrester, of Hallgarth View, aged 43. I came to know the Forrester family fairly well over the years. Mrs Forrester was left to bring up Mac, Colin and Ann, all of whom in their day were prominent in St Oswald's Church activities. And some children lost parents as a result of the war. Despite this short period of intense and puzzling sadness, by and large, my childhood was a happy one. I look back on it with gratitude, and this is what I would like to shine through. However, I would sooner not have gone through the months that followed.

Without knowing why, I was whisked out of the way and fussed over by my father's sisters, Aunts Agg and May who lived at 13 Elvet Crescent and Aunt Olive, who then lived at Bishop Auckland, where her husband Uncle Ted White was a police inspector. I even spent a very brief period with the Sayles family who ran the fish and chip shop at 46 New Elvet, roughly where the approach to the Kingsgate Bridge now stands. This was very exciting. All little boys love chips and I was able to watch as the peeling drum washed and skinned the potatoes and I helped operate the chipping machine, which deposited the finished product into spotless enamel buckets. Mr and Mrs Sayles also kept a parrot, which talked – so distraction was not too difficult.

Perhaps because TB was regarded as such a scourge in the Forties and because I also suffered from a minor imperfection of the breastbone my case came to the attention of Dr Caile (of the Claypath surgery and about whom later, incidentally, my father complained bitterly because he was unable to do anything to save my mother. Could any doctor at that time?). Dr Caile decided I should spend some time at Earl's House sanatorium, set in isolation just outside Durham on the road to Witton Gilbert.

The object, as I understand it now, was to keep an eye on me just in case anything developed. The actual details are somewhat muddled in my mind but I guess it would be only a matter of days between the death of my mother (of which I was unaware) and my admission to Earl's House. It was not a case of being rushed there by ambulance. In fact, I went by bus, from Framwelgate Waterside, accompanied by Aunt Olive who went to settle me in – though she never knew it she failed in that respect and I spent several bedridden days totally miserable and bewildered in the east wing of the sanatorium. Aunt Olive did, however, dedicate herself to my welfare while I was a patient and visited me every Saturday afternoon during my six months' "captivity." Dad made occasional "unofficial" visits when he could, sometimes turning up in fire service uniform. My questions about my mother were gently fended off, the family line being that she was in hospital, too.

For myself, I felt not the slightest bit ill. In fact, I was well enough to be a bit of a nuisance but I settled down when transferred to the West Wing where, along with a score or so other patients, I served the rest of my time. I referred to captivity because a constant subject of discussion among the lads – oddly, I cannot remember any girls being at Earl's House – was "doing a bunk." Seeing the traffic travel to and fro along the main road, just across the grounds, proved very tantalising and represented freedom. There was an oft-repeated rhyme: "East wing, West wing, Home's the best thing." But I don't think anyone made a successful home run. However, records of the county sub-committee running Earl's House through the Thirties survive at Durham Record Office and they chime very much with my memories of the place. No girl patients are referred to so I assume it was a boys-only sanatorium – where did the girls go? My own stay lasted six months but some patients were there much longer.

J. Menzies McCormack, Medical Officer, reported in 1934 that the sanatorium had an average of thirty boys in bed all day, who during their stay had no education. "Some of these boys are in bed two or three years and, in my opinion, regular teaching for these patients should be available. . ." The head teacher reported she was unable to undertake this work owing to the fact that "the difference of ages of those attending school makes it impossible to deal with them all in one class." The committee was having none of this and instructed the MO to confer with the teachers and devise a scheme for a trial period of six months. I was not confined to bed and in 1941-2 had little teaching other than just before my discharge – but by then there was a war on, you know. The talk of "doing a bunk" that I have described was obviously part of a long-held tradition among the boys. In 1934 it was reported that among the patients discharged was one with "very little hope of recovery" and another named boy who was sent home following an attempt to run away. The family of this patient complained to the sub-committee but the mother of another boy who had run away with him said she had no complaints about her son's treatment whatsoever and expressed thanks for what had been done for him.

Earl's House seems to have had between 75 and 80 patients at any one time and, as an example of the outcome of their treatment the record for September, 1936, shows 15 admissions and eight discharges and these included: one boy, aged four, who died of pulmonary TB after 41 days as a patient; one, aged 12, who was allowed home after 369 days, the disease "arrested"; and one, aged three, who was discharged after 181 days as non-tuberculous – a situation not dissimilar to my own.

Clearly the sanatorium may well have saved many young lives but, as children, we were unable to appreciate that and I can't have been the only one who did not fully understand why we were there. Occasionally, bouts of tantrums led to a culprit being restrained in a type of strait-jacket strapped to the iron bed head until he quietened down – a severe and distressing method of dealing with the situation, for victim and onlookers alike.

And there were times when the grim reality of tuberculosis was brought home to us. We would become aware that a child among us – usually one new to the ward – was really sick and we quickly grasped that the end bed near the night sister was one to be avoided. Sobbing relatives would arrive, screens arranged around the bed, and quietly, mysteriously, all would be spirited away. . .

Next day the regime would continue under the formidable Sister Bates (I think that was her name), a strapping lady. Temperature-taking, recorded on the chart at the foot of the bed; injections in the backside; inspections and stinging iodine treatment for ringworm which everyone seemed to catch, despite stringent hygiene; and regular weighings were the extent of my treatment. When the weather was fine there was plenty of fresh air on the balcony. The food was awful – offerings such as liver and tripe being particularly abhorrent to kids. The main highlights were really the distractions that occurred when visiting workmen came to fix something – or to seal and fumigate a ward with a sulphury gas. Near the end of my stay, I spent a few lessons at Earl's House school where I encountered my first struggles with Thousands, Hundreds, Tens and Units. I could already read well. In fact, I can't actually remember being taught to read; I just seem to have always been able to do it.

Earl's House's original role began as an industrial school in 1885 but from 1921 to 1953 it was a sanatorium for children and then became a hospital for handicapped children. According to the *Advertiser*, Miss Helen Appleton served Earl's House for 39 years, retiring as matron in 1969. I am certain that Miss Appleton and her staff were very dedicated and caring but any feeling of appreciation or gratitude for what they did for me is overshadowed by the fact that in my childhood bewilderment I just hated the place – and I don't think I was alone in that.

BELOW: Dad in later life with workmates at the County Police garages at Aycliffe in the late Fifties or early Sixties. He is the one in overalls, with both hands in his pockets. By then he was suffering from emphysema and was soon switched from his trade of coachpainting to driving. He suffered prolonged ill health before his retirement in 1968 and he died in October, 1972.

So, after six months, in the spring of 1942, I returned home to a much-changed situation. My father had taken in another family to help care for me. After a few days, I suppose, Dad could no longer conceal the truth and he took me along to the cemetery and, by her graveside, gently broke the news to me about Mam.

The resilience that seems to be built into children saved the day for Dad. I don't know now exactly what my feelings were but I can't remember crying. We just walked home, had our dinner and, with no further questions, I carried on with my new life. There was no Rex, either. Our fox terrier, which was by then seven or eight years old, had become a necessary casualty of the sad wartime situation.

Chapter III

SURVIVING TOMMY BARR . . .

My early education at St Oswald's School was interrupted by the death of my mother and my six-month stay at Earl's House. My memorable first day was August 28, 1940, when myself and 15 other rising-fives were added to the school's roll and placed into the tender care of Mrs Bell who gently introduced us to the great adventure of learning and getting along together. Softly spoken, with a hint of Scottish in her voice, Mrs Bell was caring but firm and effective in getting across the first principles of reading, writing and sums to a very mixed bag of infants in the "Babies" class. What she failed to get across to me on that first morning, however, was the day's timetable. As we were turned out into the school yard for playtime, I shot straight home to Highwood Terrace, believing that was it for the day. Fortunately, mother was at home and had me back at the school yard before lessons resumed.

The early lessons that made an impact on me were those involving nature study – growing peas and beans in a jam jar lined with blotting paper so that we could observe the emerging shoots and roots; growing a carrot top in a saucer of water and watching its foliage develop; and seeing cress grow from seeds on a tray of gelatine. Then there were the tadpoles, born out of frogspawn. This was fascinating stuff for kids. Mrs Bell also played the piano and sang and was a kindly mother figure, as well as an effective first mentor to all the children and I cannot recall anyone having anything but praise and admiration for her.

She lived in Boyd Street and the back gate of her home overlooked what had been, before the war, the school garden. Now it was the site of brick-built air raid shelters with reinforced concrete roofs – buildings that five years later we were fascinated to see knocked down in dramatic fashion by a swinging wrecking ball operated from a bulldozer. That really signalled the end of the war.

But Mrs Bell had a sad legacy from the First World War to contend with. Her husband

Harold had been almost completely disabled. People said it was shell shock and Mr and Mrs Bell had to cope with its sorry effects. They were often to be seen out walking – a customary recreation of the day. But Mr Bell, leaning on his wife's arm, could proceed only very slowly with a shuffling and stuttering gait and his hands and body shook with tremors not unlike Parkinson's Disease. He was always immaculately turned out and it was remarked that before his affliction he had been a man of particularly smart bearing. They would stop and pass the time of day with people they met, Mrs Bell all the while dabbing her husband's nose and mouth with a white handkerchief. They were a brave and devoted couple much admired in the community. There were no support services, as today, and Mrs Bell's loving dedication to both her sick husband and to her young charges at school were, by today's standards, nothing less than heroic.

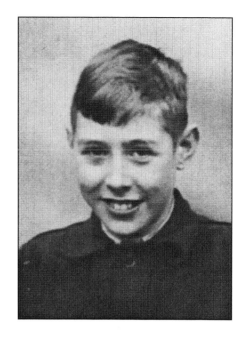

ABOVE: *No class pictures were taken at St Oswald's school while I was there, only indiviual portraits. So here I am, aged nine or ten, I guess.*

For the record, other children who started St Oswald's around the same time as myself included: Thomas Keegan, David Robinson, Audrey Owens, Florence Toase, Albert Crampton, Jimmy Brown, Ruby Spikings, Clive Titman, Dorothy Adair, Betty Owens, Frank Delap, Brian Gibson, Geoffrey Newton, Keith Cleal, Stephen Turner, Moira Keegan, Eric Robinson, Maurice Turnbull, Thomas Hazelgreaves, Paul Allison, Ann Mitchell, Sheila Tate, Joan Heron, Brian Wilson, John Craggs, Colin Shaw and Sheila Mitchinson.

Next step up the school ladder was to Head of Infants Miss Ellinor Worsnop's class. Miss Worsnop appeared to have a more traditional schoolma'am image. She lived at The Moorlands in Gilesgate and was a long-serving teacher but my personal recollection of her is less vivid because for most of that year I was at Earl's House. Then came Gertie Wilkinson, who had been appointed in 1932, and if you did not learn anything from Miss Wilkinson it was not for her want of trying.

Miss Wilkinson was a pillar of St Oswald's Church and lived with a companion, Miss Annie Davy, at Church Street Head in the house that adjoined the back lane to Highwood View. A forceful and businesslike personality, she was not slow to punish the incompetent and inattentive. Teachers then were less inhibited about backing up their authority with a bit of sting and a wooden rule would be vigorously applied to the outstretched hand of any backslider. In the case of naughty boys, an added deterrent was Miss Wilkinson's application of the ruler's edge across the knuckles. Dared you complain when you got home? Not likely. Parents were on Miss Wilkinson's side.

Miss Wilkinson moved our education on considerably with the aid of slates and slate pencils, then scratchy pens and sloppy inkpots. By the time we left her class we were able to do basic arithmetic and write in copperplate. She would carefully draught out the alphabet on the blackboard in a well-rounded hand, the ascenders and descenders and joining strokes all immaculately proportioned. The shape of the small 's', she would say, should curve like the back of a seated cat – and she would draw one on the blackboard to convince us.

This was the class in which we chanted tables till we knew them by heart; read aloud to one's classmates; and learned the importance of correct spelling. Neatness was admired and praised. Sloppy or careless work brought scathing criticism, or punishment, or both. We had moved on from being infants to juniors, ready to face a more rigorous regime. It was an important stage of our education – in effect, preparation for the real world of the day in which a smart girl or boy with good schooling and competence in the Three Rs could make their way.

At this stage, there were no tangible rewards for success but subtle incentives to do with one's status in the classroom, such as giving out or collecting in pens and pencils – simple things that conferred a modicum of importance and a sense of responsibility. You might be the one who rang the bell or blew the whistle.

It was where leadership began to emerge that was reflected in the pecking order of the playground. Where children began to look to those who were successful rather than to those who were merely loud, pushy or precocious. In today's jargon, it was how people skills were developed.

On a rough calculation of my time at St Oswald's, I must have spent two years with one teacher but I cannot now figure out which. By the time one reached Tommy Barr's classroom – upstairs overlooking the boys' yard – the dreaded Scholarship was looming. This two-part examination decided whether you would proceed to the Johnston Grammar School, still known as the Tech, the Girls' Grammar School, or Whinney Hill Secondary Modern School which, when opened in 1932, was lauded as one of the largest schools of its kind in the North East.

There was a lot of kudos in passing this exam (both educational and social) and com-

monly the incentive on offer from parents to the kids was a bicycle. The examination was what later became known as the 11-plus and if there was a debate raging at the time about whether this sort of selection was a good or bad thing we children were unaware of it – though we came to recognise that, in some cases, failure meant great disappointment for the families concerned. Miss Wilkinson may have laid a solid foundation but it was Tommy Barr and headmaster Alfred Daykin who prepared us for this great ordeal.

Mr Barr lived in School House, just behind the school in School Lane, with his wife and three daughters, Molly, Joan and Nona (Winona). He was widely known in the community but among children his reputation as a stern disciplinarian with a heavy hand over-shadowed his undoubted teaching skills.

He could certainly keep order in a large class of varied talents and backgrounds but it is equally certain that his severe methods would not be regarded as acceptable today. Physical punishment was liberally dispensed to the boys by means of a vicious cuff round the ear and his loud voice was also used effectively to keep the class in order. He could be scathing about the turn-out or lack of cleanliness of some of the poorer children and he was merciless towards some of those who came from Sherburn Road Estate – referring sarcastically to that area as the forest (its various avenues being named after trees, oak, ash, laurel etc.). If you could survive all that you could also learn something from Tommy Barr. In addition to academic subjects, he used to take us for games in the schoolyard, mostly comprising team relay races, sometimes with wooden hoops. We also went on nature walks led by him, for example along School Lane, up Mount Joy Hill, through Little High Wood and back to school via South Road and the New Inn.

By the time I arrived with Mr Barr, of course, the war was at its end. Occasionally, there were gifts of fruit, chocolate or cocoa powder from Canada and, though it was late in the war in 1944 there were evacuees from the Barnet area, presumably to escape from the V1 and V2 flying bombs that the Germans were raining on London.

A party of 12 children arrived, apparently organised by Miss Doris Sadler, a wealthy stalwart of St Oswald's Church, who lived at Oswald House, an imposing property in South Road, at the end of Hollingside Lane, where Collingwood College now stands. Miss Sadler, a rather tweedy figure, lived with her mother Mrs Amy Sadler, widow of Cecil James Sadler, who died in 1936. He had been chairman of a Teesside chemical company. I am sure Miss Sadler's involvement with evacuees was part of her community war effort. In any event, the children arrived, were billeted with local families, including the Sadlers themselves, were duly mocked for their "Cockney" accents but settled in well and returned home safely only a few months later when the war was over.

Children's welfare was a high priority during the war and afterwards and we received free school milk – in winter the crates of third-pint bottles was often warmed in front the the classroom's large coal fire. And there were school dinners in the downstairs hall delivered by van in insulated metal containers from a central kitchen in Framwelgate.

Part of the Monday morning ritual at school was handing in 2s 1d for dinners (5d a day for me – 4d a day each if there were two schoolchildren from one family and pro rata down to free dinners for the very poorest). I also paid 6d a week for a National Savings stamp. Once this had accumulated to a pound, or a guinea, the money was converted into a Savings Certificate. This scheme was a big part of the war effort and every part of town had a war savings committee.

By the time Scholarship year came round I was living at the shop in Hallgarth Street run by my stepmother Florrie. She was ambitious for me and, concerned that I had missed some schooling earlier, sent me for coaching to Mr Heatley, head of the village school at Croxdale, whose mother lived to a ripe old age in Highwood View. I made only two or three visits and he quickly came to the conclusion that there was nothing to worry about and I should be accomplished enough to pass the examination.

The year was 1947 – one which has gone down in history as a very bad winter. There were heavy snowfalls and, to the delight of all children, schools were closed for a while. The Scholarship was postponed. The first half, sat in one's own schools, was a qualifying exam and consisted of English and arithmetic papers. This was taken in Mr Daykin's classroom and, to ensure the candidates' concentration was not broken, the rest of the school had the day off. I tried to acquire copies of the examinations we sat to demonstrate the level of education we were required to reach by the age of 11 in the 1940s and to compare it to the computer and calculator-aided standard of today. But to no avail: the county records office has no such papers. However, Mary Almond, of Highwood View, a self-confessed hoarder of all family trifles, has ridden to the rescue and come up with the 1951 "first-half" papers taken by her brother Edward, now head of the family plumbing company. They are reproduced at the end of this book, for readers to have a go (answers are not provided).

What surprises me now is not so much their content but the speed with which we had to complete the exams – 45 minutes each for English (four questions, including a tough comprehension piece) and Arithmetic (seven problems). Try them.

The post-examination wait was a tense one for pupils and families – at least for those who cared. There was a significant minority who did not; and some who simply took a realistic view of their chances and looked forward to moving on to Whinney Hill school. However, a good number passed the first half and then it was off to the grammar schools to sit the second half, a competitive intelligence and aptitude test.

I was among a group of boys who took their test in the art room at the Johnston Grammar School in South Street. It had very large windows, was on the top floor, contained classical-style statues, including a discus thrower, and was in the wing of the school whose imposing gable made an impressive sight from Framwelgate Bridge. The tests took all day, we had dinner at the school, and felt very important – but many would never cross its portals again.

The *Durham Advertiser* for Friday, June 13th, 1947 (unlucky for some) records:
GRAMMAR SCHOOL SUCCESSES

In the admission examinations for county grammar schools, there was a total of 1,471 places available. The number of pupils taking the qualifying examination was 13,151. The following, who have qualified for admission, are recommended for special places:

K. Allport, K. Aston, W.L. Bean, P.S. Bone, W. Bowyer, M. Brennan, R. Chicken, G. E. Clark, S. Coulson, **T. E. Coulson**, R.R. Cowley, C. R. Dixon, W.K. Dunning, J. Elliott, D.W. Forster, F. Gardiner, H. Gill, W. Harrod, **P.W. Hempson**, D. Henderson, J. R. Henderson, M. A. Hill, K. Humm, N.J. Kinnear, B. Leightell, J.T. Little, B. Littleton, K. Metcalfe, B. McDermott, K.J. McGuire, M.McKenna, J. Naylor, G.K. Nimmins, T.W.K Noyes, J. E. Nunn, N.P. O'Donnell, K. Oliver, N. Oliver, J.T. Ord, K. Parkinson, C. Pinkney, P. Rawlinson, B. Robertson, T. W.

Rutherford, W. Scarr, I.C. Shepherd, J. Standring, M. Stewart, T. H. Stoddart, C. Sudder, W. Suddess, W. Thompson, W. Tilley, C. W. Titman, J. A. Tomlinson, T. M. Trotter, G. A. Watson, A. E. Watts, J.K. Wheatley, J. W. Wiggam, A. D. Wilson, A. Young, **D. Young**, H. Young. (64 names; those in bold are St Oswald's boys. Clive Titman, who lived at my former home 4 Highwood Terrace, Terence Coulson from the prison officers' houses on Whinney Hill, and myself were bosom pals at that time).

DURHAM GIRLS' GRAMMAR SCHOOL

Mary E. Allen, Rita Allen, Patricia Allison, **Doreen J. Blackett**, Enid I. Caiger, Joyce Campy, June Carlin, Margaret Chappell, Ann Clark, Muriel Corbett, Louisa E. Cousin, Jean Dodds, Ann Embleton, Anne Field, Joyce C. Gillson,, Dorothy Gilmore, Renee Glew, Lillian Graham, Anne C. Gustard, Mary P. Hannah, Mary J. Hogarth, Mavis Humble, Jean M. Jackson, Margaret S. Jarrett, Margaret Kennedy, Ann Kerwin, Joan. E. Kidd, Joan W. Kipling, Mary Knight, Doreen Law, Dorothy Lawson, Mary E. Lee, Lilian G, Lowery, Janet I. Lush, Elizabeth K. Lynn, Audrey Marshall, Rosamund J. Mercer, Enid Mitchell, Margaret Nicholson, Constance Palmer, Rae Parkinson, Rosalin Pearson, Elizabeth H. Prowse, Aileen E. Robinson, Dorothy S. Robson, Patricia Ryans, Patricia E.Scott, Janet Shanks, Irene Simpson, Anne Skellett, Alice M. Smith, Gwyneth Smith, Jean Stainthorpe, Vera Stockdale, Margaret Tait, Audrey Tidbury, Dorothy Ann Truby, Pauline Truscott, Marion Vasey, Joyce Walker, Hillary Wallace, Mary M. Willson, Evelyn Wise, Benita Yard, Joyce Gibbons (65 girls named).

Even in a period of post-war austerity, St Oswald's School, was generous in its prize-giving and to this day I possess *The Moonstone* by Wilkie Collins for my scholarship success in 1947. Earlier prizes were *Queer Fish* for Merit, Christmas 1945; and *The Wonders of Coal*, Christmas 1946 "Presented to David Young by Mr Ternent for Composition." I trust the present reader will not conclude that Mr Ternent's generosity was misplaced. All the prizes were inscribed by Headmaster Mr Alfred Daykin himself in a wonderfully neat hand. Mr W.H. Ternent was then a retired teacher, whose connections with the Johnston school stretched back to 1902. His home, with his sister, Miss K. Ternent, was a cottage with a walled garden, a few yards along Stockton Road from the New Inn.

* * *

What are little boys made of? Slugs and snails and puppy dogs' tails.
What are little girls made of? Sugar and spice and all things nice.

Though things began to change in the war, these nursery rhyme metaphors essentially still held true. Boys were rough, girls were gentle. Boys were dirty and untidy, girls were neat and tidy. Boys did gardening and woodwork, girls did housework and needlework. Daddies went to work, mammies stayed at home. This list of perceived differences was clearcut and almost endless and was the accepted way of the world.

It was the basis of the etiquette of the day. "Ladies before gentlemen." "Raise your cap to the lady, David," my father would say. In any crowded situation boys would give up their seats to girls, men to ladies. Sometimes the deference to the fair sex might be a bit grudging (we were no angels) but in general, it ruled the day. "Manners makyth man" was an oft-repeated epigram, usually delivered as a rebuke for some lapse, and while many of the conventions hold true today, one area where modern lifestyle shows many changes is in our attitudes to death and funerals.

The girls' side of St Oswald's School Yard was situated next to School Lane, which ran from Church Street, passed the school and School House to the gates of the Stockton Road cemetery. Many children's first brush with death, so to speak, would be to see a funeral passing along this lane. The cortege from the church would pass by with the coffin being carried by bearers, followed by walking mourners and sympathisers, almost invariably dressed in black – even in wartime. If it should pass by at playtime, or during a PT session, the reaction of the children was respectful and immediate. Everyone would stand still, remain silent with heads bowed, and boys would remove their caps. Furthermore, we were taught to behave in a similar manner should we encounter a hearse in the street. And we did!

I was not at my own mother's funeral (being regarded as too young for such a distressing ordeal) but Ethel Pickering (née Dunn) remembers her father's as a ten-year-old in February, 1944. James Robert Dunn, of 25 Hallgarth Street, sadly died at the age of 54 only a week after being taken ill. A Sherburn Hill colliery worker, he left a widow, four sons and three daughters. Ethel and Elsie were more or less my contemporaries but their brothers included older twins, Thomas and Joseph, both serving in the Durham Light Infantry, with all the anxiety this entailed for a family in wartime. Ethel remembers that the family followed the coffin from home to church on foot.

When someone died the bereaved household's curtains would be kept closed, and on the day of the funeral all the neighbours would close their curtains, too, until the ceremony was over as a mark of respect. By contrast with some of today's pop-culture sentimental secular funerals, the old Prayer Book version that generations had grown up with – and in many cases were sadly only too familiar with – had a solemnity that reflected people's sense of loss but at the same time offered hope.

The customs we grew up with had remained unchanged for years, echoes of a more respectful age. Amid today's hurly-burly, if observed at all, they would pass virtually unnoticed. Though it is interesting, in a slightly different context, that under pressure from the older generation, the Armistice Day two-minutes' silence is making its way back into general acceptance.

Chapter IV

WHAT, RABBIT AGAIN?

After Earl's House I must have spent two wartime Christmases at Highwood Terrace. Of course, I received the traditional Christmas stocking which reflected Christmases of my parents' childhood – an apple an orange and two or three shiny new pennies in the toe. In addition, there were toys, books and games bringing a feeling of general well-being and happiness. One became conscious, then, of the war being acted out in kids' play. Cowboys and Indians or Cops and Robbers were commonplace but frequently developed into fighting the Germans. Cap pistols were popular but if there was nothing to hand we played with imaginary weapons – the hand being formed into a pistol shape with the fore-finger and middle finger representing the barrel which was pointed at the "foe" with accompanying noises. "Peeow, cheeow, Got yer, you're dead." "No ah'm not. Yer missed" was the invariable riposte. So battle continued. No one vanquished. No one victorious. No one hurt.

Imagine the joy, then, when one Christmas some hand-made toys made by a craftsman in the fire service arrived. In 1944, the *Advertiser* recorded thanks to the NFS for making toys during their rest hours that were to be sold in aid of the service's benevolent fund and I was not the only child to receive a wooden tommy-gun with a handle and ratchet to pro-duce a realistic rat-tat-tat. Out in the street with those we must have sent the neighbour-hood mad and, had there been any around at the time, the Germans would have been in hotfoot retreat. Many toys were militaristic – wooden tanks, ships and aeroplanes. Indeed it must have been the era when aero-modelling first took off. All young boys had heard of Spitfires, Hurricanes and Messerschmidts and this interest was fed by the propaganda and Government campaigns of the day.

On one occasion a shot-down German aircraft was put on display in the Market Place. Not much to see in reality but it was still an object of fascination, drawing small crowds who would simply stand and stare for a few minutes before moving on. An empty old shop in Saddler Street was often used for pictorial displays along with exhortations to support the war effort through National Savings. A large bomb would be on display and people were encouraged to buy a sixpenny savings stamp to stick on it as Hitler's birthday or Christmas present. There were Spitfire Weeks, Battleship Weeks, Salute the Soldier Weeks and endless campaigns keeping the war effort at the forefront of people's minds and keeping the money rolling in. Spy paranoia abounded. "Careless talk costs lives" was a prominent slogan.

Meanwhile on the Klondike allotments gardeners were "Digging for Victory", and at home housewives had to learn not only how to make something palatable out of dried egg and other meagre rations but how to "Make Do and Mend", to eke out threadbare clothing. Mothballs were a vital part of this armoury.

Rationing might have been inconvenient and unpopular, and there were undoubtedly huge black-market evasions, but in retrospect the diet we were forced to live on proved a healthy one. However, everyone looked forward to there being unlimited best butter, sugar, cream, and meat with plenty of fat on it. They felt they'd earned it.

Going to Durham indoor market for rabbits was a Saturday morning ritual and the seemingly endless permutations for serving it up – roast, pie, stew, potted meat – put me off it for the rest of my life.

* * *

One of the sacrifices of the war evident to this day was the removal of decorative iron railings from property frontages. All the houses in Highwood Terrace and Highwood View had dwarf walls in front of their bay windows – and still have. These walls were embellished with quite plain tubular iron rails which, it was deemed, were needed to help the war effort. Indeed all over Britain buildings were stripped of these elegant features. Very few appear to have been replaced and it is said now that they were of little significant use. Their removal in the war's dark days were an indication to the populace that "something was being done " – as was the collection of old metal pots and pans, which is also said to have proved of little value. When it was Highwood Terrace's turn, a team of two or three workmen with oxy-acetylene cutting equipment arrived to set about the work.

For children this was an exciting spectacle with sparks flying and metal glowing white hot, so throughout their endeavours the men were followed by a small audience of local kids. It's a very trivial thing to have stuck in one's mind for so long but when a gas cylinder became exhausted a workman chalked the letters MT on it. "What does that mean?" one of us asked. The workmen just laughed and teased us about not being able to read properly. 'MT' was their code for 'Empty.'

Men at work would always draw a crowd, especially when there was spectacular equipment involved. When the road was re-surfaced, tar would be melted and sprayed, chippings would be spread and consolidated by a steam roller puff-puffing back and forth with flywheel spinning and chimney belching smoke. While past its heyday, steam was somewhat reprieved by the war and traction engines and steam lorries continued in service beyond their natural lifespan. Indeed, I can clearly remember a steam dray delivering to the Hare & Hounds on Elvet Bank. In late summer a threshing team would pass by between farms, two or three huge trailers being hauled by the types of traction engine that are fascinating museum pieces today. Horses, too, had an important role. On Mount Joy farm they were still used, along with an old Fordson tractor, to haul reaper and binder at harvest time and to carry away loads of potatoes in the autumn picking season. In the streets, flat carts run by dealers Ambrose Appleby of Elvet and Newtons of Gilesgate, were a familiar sight. And Rington's Tea vans were like Hansom cabs with two large cartwheels. A sad experience was to see a horse, fallen in its shafts, destroyed near Anchorage House and hauled up in tarpaulin on to the Spennymoor fellmonger's lorry. On the brighter side, manure did not stand long in the quieter streets. There'd be someone out quickly with bucket and shovel, thinking of their roses! Horse fairs also survived for a while after the war, outside the Assize Courts, between Court Lane and Old Elvet. Horse dealers, gipsies and spectators would gather to watch the animals being trotted through their paces and deals being done with a spit and a handshake – a very colourful but, by then, outdated spectacle.

* * *

Early in 1944 my father remarried. His bride was "local girl" Florrie Butterfield who had been born in 1903 (daughter of an upholsterer who worked for Pattinsons) and brought up in Boyd Street and who then lived in a flat in Church Street Head. She had worked for many years as a shop assistant at Fred Docherty's, the tailors, in Saddler Street and had been a friend of my mother. An old family album shows that Florrie had been a member of the City amateur operatic society before the war and she spoke of being a fire-watcher in the early years of the war. They were married at St Cuthbert's Church, off Old Elvet, by Father Meagher, Florrie having "turned Catholic" at some point, possibly under the influence of her elder sister Mary who had by then married and lived in the woollen mill town of Keighley, West Yorkshire.

Faced with yet another change of direction I recall being somewhat truculent and resentful with Florrie at first, though she worked hard and devotedly to bring me up well. She took great pride in my achievements and encouraged me in activities where Dad's instincts were inclined to be over-protective.

ABOVE: Members of the chorus in an amateur operatic society production in Durham in the late Twenties or early Thirties. My stepmother, then Florrie Butterfield (front left, seated), and her friends were enthusiastic members. Can anyone name the show and supply names?

A legal wrangle, when father wanted to re-possess the full tenancy of 4 Highwood Terrace from the family brought in to look after me, resulted in the no-win compromise of both families having to move out and we found our-selves in Dixon's general dealers in Hallgarth Street, a small shop at the end of Mavin Street, opposite the Victoria Inn. On a recent visit I was astonished to find that it is now an Italian restaurant.

The property was extremely run-down and mice-infested. It lacked even the minimal facilities of Highwood Terrace. Lighting was by gas, cooking was by an old-fashioned black-leaded Victorian range, water came from a single tap in the corner of the living room – but there was no drain, slops having to be carried across Mavin Street's cobbles and poured into the nearest open drain. The toilet was an outhouse even farther up Mavin Street, as were a coalhouse and a wash-house with its coal boiler. It was all rather Dickensian, but not unlike other corners of the city that had been left behind when slum clearance was under way in the Thirties.

The fact is that Elvet ward had a pretty grim and long-standing record of deprivation. In 1849, a General Health Board report on the area described "back courts, lanes and alleys inhabited almost exclusively by the poorer classes with a prevalence of open privies and piggeries, many of them of the most noxious and filthy description." Of course, during the following 100 years sanitation and general hygiene improved beyond measure but there were still pockets of private property in the late Forties and early Fifties that by the modest standards of the day were nothing less than a disgrace.

In 1951, Jean O'Connor, not long wed, began to bring up her family in rooms in Church Street (where Oswald Court now stands) at a rent of 8s. a week. She recalls: "There were no fewer than nine families in the property. It was still lit by gas and we all shared only two outside loos, along with the tenants of two neighbouring cottages."

It is worth noting that the landlord was the much-honoured city Alderman John Willy Pattinson, of the Dunelm Café and Hotel in Old Elvet; a Salvation Army supporter and former Mayor, who had the honorary freedom of the city

ABOVE Dad and Florrie pictured in the early 50s in the garden of 70 Hallgarth Street where they lived after leaving the shop.

conferred upon him in 1950. Nicknamed "Rammer," but I don't know why, Ald Pattinson, a baker with a finger in most city pies, liked the civic limelight and while his achievements in certain fields may have been significant it would have been scant consolation for his tenants.

In Hallgarth Street around this time there were quite a mixture of properties ranging from slum tenements down passageways to some quite grand houses, one of the deprived areas being High Yard, off Church Lane.

Back at No 17, where we were making a new beginning, electric lighting, a modern range and a gas cooker were installed as soon as practicable after the war so it became quite cosy, but bitterly cold in winter. Though its address was Hallgarth Street, the house entrance was in Mavin Street and the living room's sash window had shutters, as did the shop frontage, which were made full use of to help keep out both the cold and burglars.

My bedroom was above the shop, overlooking Hallgarth Street, with the Victoria inn right opposite. There was a gas lamp outside, which remained unlit until after the war. I could lie abed, almost recognising the footsteps of the various people passing to and fro and, just before 10pm, Mr Petrie's voice at the Vic would rise above everything : "Time gentlemen, please." Animated conversations begun in the pub would continue for a while on the pavement outside but by twenty past it was all over. Most people were well in bed by

BELOW: This is my favourite picture. Craftsmen from a different era taken at a coach and carriageworks somewhere at the foot of Elvet around the turn of the 19th/20th Century. My grandfather, Arthur Young, was a journeyman coachpainter, as was my father, and is seen resting his arm on the wheel of the gig. According to my father, Grandfather was ginger-haired and possessed a temper to match that landed him in trouble with his bosses more than once. Arthur Young died at St Oswald's School House, Church Street, in 1927, aged 55.

then and the night would descend into a hush, broken only by the occasional puffing and whistling of a distant train and, of course, by the Cathedral chiming every quarter. Even without an illuminated alarm clock by the bedside, the Cathedral and the Westminster chimer on the sideboard downstairs kept one well in touch with the hour on a restless night.

Next door in Mavin Street lived an old lady called Anne Kennerel, known as Miss, which mystified me because from time to time she had a visitor who was said to be her son. Miss Kennerel caused us much amusement when electricity was installed. Dad asked her how she was getting on with it and she replied: "Wonderful, I can now see much better to light my lamps." Even with gas on tap she had persisted with her oil lamps and new-fangled electricity wasn't going to change anything. Indeed Parker, the lamp oil man from Gilesgate, was still a familiar figure in the streets with his horse and cart and later with his van, selling paraffin for lighting and heating. Opposite lived the elderly brothers and sisters Mary and Annie Baker. The two men both had moustaches, wore flat caps and white silk scarves, smoked clay pipes and sported pocket watches and chains in their waistcoats. One of them, Billy, could almost always be seen at the bottom of Elvet watching the world go by outside the Half Moon Hotel.

Moving to Hallgarth Street was for dad and me a return to the roots from which many of the extensive Young family in Durham flowered. The Youngs occupied a number of houses in the street in the early 1900s, moving from one to another as the number of off-spring increased. Nos. 35, 37, 92 where dad was born, and 15 were among their dwellings.

Arthur Young, coach painter, and his wife Mary Jane (née Bailes, of Framwelgate) had eleven children altogether. The first-born Agnes (there was a later Agnes) died, aged five, in 1900 and George, aged five months, died in 1908. So my father William Henry, known as Harry (the fifth child, born in 1903) and his four brothers and four sisters grew up and led, full, respectable and fruitful lives as did many of the poorer families of those days. Eldest was Arthur, born 1897. He married Annie Sheldon Smith at Old Elvet Wesleyan Church and they eventually moved to the south of England where Uncle Arthur was in service as a gentleman's gentleman. They had a son Kenneth, who served in the Navy during the war and who went on to own his own garage business, and twin daughters Joan and Jean.

Next came Aunt Olive, born 1899. Margaret (Aunt Meg) was born in 1901 and, as a young lady, worked at Madam Gray's the ladies' fashion shop in North Road. She and her husband Tom Broughton (of pop factory family) spent most of their working lives at Carlisle where she ran a corner shop and he was a plasterer. He was also a musician, a tal-

ABOVE: 26th September, 1923: After the wedding at St Oswald's church of my aunt Olive Pring Young to Edward Horace (Ted) White, a policeman and Durham City CC fast bowler. On the left are my paternal grandparents, Arthur, a coachpainter, and Mary Jane (née Bailes, of Framwelgate), who at that time lived at 15 Hallgarth Street. She bore 11 children in the 17 years between 1895 and 1912, of whom Aunt Olive was the third (b1899). As a girl, Olive had worked at Woodcock's grocery shop at the foot of Hallgarth Street. On the right bridesmaid Margaret Young (Aunt Meg) was the fourth child (b1901). Best Man is James Nunn, about whom I know nothing except that he may have been a police colleague of Uncle Ted, a Londoner, who at the time was living at 17 Boyd Street.

The Whites lived at West Auckland, Bishop Auckland and Birtley before Uncle Ted retired as an inspector. They then spent a short period running a pub in a Cambridgeshire village before, inevitably, returning to Durham to manage a wine shop in the Market Place with living accommodation above. Next, they moved to Back Mount Joy and in the early Fifties Uncle Ted saw out his working career at Elvet House. Their son , my cousin Harry (named after my father), served in the army in Germany towards the end of the war and later moved South in a civil service job. But he did for some years keep in touch with his Elvet pal Bill Shotton, of Whinney Hill. Aunt Olive collapsed and died while shopping in Greenwell's in Silver Street in 1985. By then she and her husband were living in a flat more or less where High Yard used to be, off Church Lane.

My grandfather died at St Oswald's School House on April 5, 1927, aged 55, and my grandmother at 48a New Elvet on September 7, 1931, aged 56 – four years before I was born. Chronic nephritis (kidney failure) figures on both death certificates. Was this just a coincidence, or was it a common cause of death at that time?

The picture by J.S. Adamson, City Studio, 69 Saddler Street, Durham, might have been taken by the side of St Oswald's Institute – a rather drab setting compared with today's elaborate wedding studies.

ented oboist and played at his local theatre. On retirement in the 1960s they came to live in Gladstone Villas, later moving to a smaller house in Mount Joy Crescent. After Uncle Tom died Aunt Meg first went to a residential home in Allergate, then to Sherburn House where she spent her last days. Their son Eric served in the Royal Canadian Air Force and continued there in civil engineering. Next after my father came Eliza May (Aunt May), born in 1904. More about her later.

Thomas Layton Young (Uncle Tom), born in 1906, married Mary Bilton in the '30s and became a leading figure in motor engineers Fowler and Armstrong in Potters Bank and later at their premises in Dragonville. Uncle Tom and Aunt Mary lived at Warwick Court, Merry Oaks, and were prominent in Durham City Golf Club.

Agnes Young (1907), named after the deceased firstborn, was a lively and generous personality who spent part of the war working in London. On her return she worked as secretary at McIntyre's garage in Elvet run by brothers John and Billy McIntyre. She was in her late forties when she married widower John McIntyre in 1955. He was a prominent city councillor and the pair were also

ABOVE RIGHT & RIGHT: Young men about town Uncle Walter (left) and Uncle Jack, with their sister Aunt Agg, in a separate study, taken in the back garden of 48a New Elvet, long since demolished. Uncle Walter was a designer at the Durham carpet factory of Hugh Mackay and Uncle Jack was a motor mechanic with Fowler and Armstrong in New Elvet. Later the unmarried members of the family moved to 13 Elvet Crescent, across the road. In the 1950s, Aunt Agg married widower, city councillor and garage proprietor John McIntyre and lived in Quarry Heads Lane until her death in the early 90s.

playing members of the private Durham City Bowling Club on the racecourse. They lived in Quarry Heads Lane until Aunt Agg died in 1992.

John Young (Uncle Jack, 1910) also spent a lifetime with Fowler and Armstrong in Elvet, first at the old garage backing on to the river and later at the modern new premises on the corner of Court Lane. In 1942, he married Mary McIntyre (for many years a supervisor at Woolworth's in Durham) at St Patrick's Church, Langley Moor, and they lived in Langley Moor for the rest of their lives. There is a daughter Christine, who became a schoolteacher. And finally, Uncle Walter was born in 1912. He made his career as a carpet designer at Mackay's factory, married Bertha Britton, of Framwelgate, at St Cuthbert's Church in 1940 and served in the RAF during the war. They lived in the very steep Neville Street, off North Road, after their daughter Wendy was born, later moving to a new city council house in Sunderland Road, near Rollings shop. There is also a son Colin.

So these were all products of humble Hallgarth Street, the family leaving to live in St Oswald's School House and, after their father died, to 48a New Elvet, where their mother died. I had often wondered how my grandparents came to move from Hallgarth Street to School House (where my father remembered keeping bantams) but the mystery was solved by Peggy Davies (aged 92, of The Hallgarth) ex-landlady of the Three Hearts of Gold, who has a clear recollection of grandfather being school caretaker.

The next move was to a modern council house, 13 Elvet Crescent, home to my father, Uncles Tom, Jack and Walter (until they married), Aunt Agg and Aunt May.

Auntie May was in a way an exception in that she was tragically struck down by mental illness in middle age and though her life thereafter was pretty miserable even she was 70 when she died at Winterton Hospital, Sedgefield, in 1974. When Auntie May was taken ill in the early 1950s there was still a stigma surrounding mental illness and being "sent to Sedgefield." Her siblings were deeply upset, my father particularly being in denial.

I was surprised to learn – though there had been some clear indications of her mental instability – that Auntie May, the gentle aunt, the one who always reminded me to say my prayers, might be violent. She was certified and forcibly taken to Winterton, an unpleasant business involving the presence of a magistrate and a doctor.

Auntie May had been the old-fashioned one of the family in dress and ways, always conscientious and considerate of others. She worked at Coyne's, the drapers in Saddler Street, and her discovery of the body of the proprietor, who had tragically hanged himself, was felt by the family to have sparked off her mental decline. Later she worked briefly at the National Health Pricing Bureau, then in New Elvet, by the corner of Court Lane.

Auntie May was a devout worshipper at St Oswald's and with her physically-handicapped friend Joan Rose, who also lived locally, maintained an interest in the Girls' Friendly Society well into adulthood. I think this is the same Joan Rose who appeared in a 1913 photograph of staff and patients at Sherburn House featured in Michael F. Richardson's book *Around Durham*.

A pang of conscience here – Auntie Agg, Auntie Olive and Auntie Meg took on the responsibility of visiting Auntie May during her long stay at Winterton but so far as I know none of her nephews nor nieces ever did. I last saw her when she had a short spell at home in the late Fifties. Part of her early treatment was the horrific electro-convulsive therapy, which to the lay person was pretty much akin to torture. How such an outwardly gentle soul endured this is difficult to imagine. (Blessed are the meek for they shall inherit the earth, indeed.)

* * *

13 Elvet Crescent is on the corner of New Elvet, facing south towards the junction of Church Street and Hallgarth Street. After their brothers married, Aunt Agg and Aunt May continued to live there and I was a frequent visitor to this highly-polished pristine house (many times for a hot bath) which often became the scene of family get-togethers in the late Forties.

Early in the war the authorities spotted its possibility as a machine-gun post and bricks were knocked out from under the front bedroom window, ready for action, and the holes simply papered over. It conjured in my mind as a child images of snipers picking off Germans as they advanced down the bank from Church Street into New Elvet. Aunt Agg always complained about the draught and, for the duration, the room became a sitting room, complete with piano and china cabinet, rather than a bedroom and it was used only on high days and holidays – usually family reunions at Christmas and New Year.

Chapter V

THE GANG'S ALL HERE

After an appeal in the *Durham Advertiser*, in August, 1999, for information which might help me with this narrative I received the following from Mrs Win Colman, of Church Villas, Church Street Head:

"Your memories of St Oswald's parish, like mine, were of a very active and happy place, especially for those of us who were youngsters and teenagers there and then. . .The great times we had as Scouts and Guides and members of the church were largely due to Hilary Morse, the Vicar, and his wife Theresa. He died many years ago but Theresa lives in the Lake District and I keep in touch with her.

"I'm still very involved with young people and the church but things are not as they were in 'our day.' There are very few youngsters living in the parish and now many residents are either pensioners or students – not the families of the Forties, Fifties, and Sixties.

"The same applies to the school,which is thriving, though most of the children come from quite far away."

When I was a child Win was Winifred Slater, of Back Mount Joy, a couple of years older so, therefore, not one of my immediate circle of friends. She was, however, a Guide, when I was in Cubs and Scouts and was a familiar figure, taking a leading role in Gang Shows, church parades and so on. Along with Sunday School, the choir and Youth Fellowship, these things were the stuff of life for many youngsters in the parish. It all began at St Oswald's, a church school, of course.

The school's ethos in the Forties was still pretty much as set out in a *Durham Advertiser* report when the remodelled St Oswald's was opened in 1932. The then Vicar, the Rev Alexander Dunn, recounted how the school's improvements came about:

"Partly, it is the result of a democracy which has clothed our poorest people with a new importance and a new dignity so that they insist, and rightly insist, upon the child of the poorest citizen being regarded as an important asset in the life of the nation.

"Partly, I think, it is the growth among Christian people of a worthier sense of duty towards the little ones of Christ. This new sense of the dignity and importance of the child is not limited to the Christian. The enemy is seeking to uproot Christianity by destroying the family and so handling the child as to destroy the very elements of morality and religion.

"We may, therefore, rejoice we have State schools set up, in our midst. We may well thank God that we have in this parish children in their earliest years who shall be taught the fundamental principles upon which the whole fabric of good living must prevail, and, far more than that, shall be brought in those sensitive years into the atmosphere of Christian influence and into contact with Christian teachers and friends. We may, therefore, be very jealous for our church schools which embody this imperilled principle of religious education."

In retrospect, I feel that it was the impression that St Oswald's catered for poor children that led to some middle-class families sending their offspring to such schools as Western Hill, the Blue Coat and the Model. I don't think the standard of education provided could be seriously faulted, though.

In the Forties, the Rev. Alexander Dunn's successor, the Rev. Hilary B. Morse, was a familiar figure in the classrooms and, as pupils, we were taken to church on key festivals each year. The most memorable to me was Ash Wednesday when each member of the congregation in a solemn ceremony was given an individual blessing and a mark of ash on the forehead administered by the Vicar's thumb. The mark remained there for the rest of the day and sometimes till next day – for some of us boys were not as scrupulous with the soap and water as we might have been.

Other high days and holidays were celebrated at school including May Day (I have vague memories of girls dancing round a maypole in the school yard) and Empire Day where flags and costumes representing the countries and peoples of the Empire were involved. Empire Day and Royal Oak Day (marking Charles II's restoration to the Throne) were both in May, one on the 24th the other the 29th, and children had a little chant: "The 29th of May is Oak Apple Day. If we don't get a holiday we'll all run away." There was also the tradition of the Cathedral choir ascending the central tower and singing anthems from three of its four corners.

Such influences as these, along with the parental background and experience in what was then a fairly static and traditional community, led many children into church organisations. And, so it was, after we had settled in Hallgarth Street, my father took me to join the choir. We had only a few yards to walk, across the road, up Church Lane, across Church Street, and we were there. We were let in by the Vicar's maid, Lena, and taken into the first room on the left looking out on to Church Street. The Vicar (who the children called "Skip", as in Skipper Morse, Scout leader) asked : "What are we going to sing?"

"There is a green hill far away, without a city wall."

He played the piano and I struggled through a couple of verses and up and down the scales and I was given a chance. On my first Sunday, I donned the black cassock (but not a surplice) to indicate my status as probationer and began to learn the various moves which ensured you arrived at the correct choir stall on entry to the church from the vestry or after processions. Miss Margaret Atack, of Mount Joy Crescent, a red-haired lady, was organist and choirmistress then, and on choir practice nights would run us through the forthcoming Sunday's hymns and any particularly tricky passages in the psalms or whatever. Though it was always difficult for me, I enjoyed the music and do to this day. Parish Communion and Evensong were the two services we sung for and part of the duties were putting up the hymn and psalm numbers on the boards in the church and removing them afterwards. Many a time the congregation was misled by our mistakes.

It was inevitable I ran into trouble, however, because I couldn't sing. My voice was flat. With the Vicar's wedding in April, 1944, rapidly approaching and a tricky anthem by the choir a central feature of it, I was omitted from the choral line-up. My permanent departure from the choir stalls was not too long delayed. But some highlights have stayed with me. Harvest Festival, for example, with a well-decorated church and the usual hymns lustily belted out by choir and packed congregation alike: "We plough the fields and scatter the good seed on the land." Even in wartime and the shortages immediately thereafter there was always a wonderful display of the generous gifts of produce and flowers, particularly chrysanthemums, which local allotment holders took a pride in growing. Then, after evensong, came an exciting ride on the Vicar's open Lagonda, cassocks and surplices flapping in the wind down Shincliffe Peth, to the little mission church at Houghall where the service, to the accompaniment of harmonium, was repeated for the agricultural college families and the residents of the few remaining cottages of the former village colliery.

Another great occasion was Ascension Day when the choir, Cubs, Scouts and Guides and other members of the congregation would board the Express's best coaches for the trip

to Finchale Abbey – an annual pilgrimage for an afternoon's play among the ruins, picnic and the service of evensong. Robed clergy and choir made a splendid sight in the abbey ruins on a fine day and, of course, children who had travelled little in wartime enjoyed the adventure. We sang Ten Green Bottles and other favourites on the bus home – and gave little thought to the hermit St Godric in whose honour the occasion was held. There was also a Rogationtide "beating the bounds" type of ceremony which took

ABOVE The annual Ascension Day pilgrimage to Finchale Abbey was a feature of St Oswald's church life, popular among the young for it included a picnic and the opportunity to play among the abbey ruins and by the river before Evensong. This 1952 procession was led by Crucifer Mr F. Kny-Jones.

The two churchwardens were Arthur Almond (left), head of the Highwood View plumbing firm, and Mr Billy McIntyre, of Mount Joy Crescent, joint proprietor of McIntyre's garage in New Elvet.

us round the fields of Mount Joy Farm. Activities like these – plus experiences in Cubs, Scouts, Sunday School and Youth Fellowship – moulded kids of the parish into reasonably responsible and well-behaved young people, though far from perfect, of course. There was always a surge in Sunday School attendance by the opportunists in the few weeks before the Christmas party in the school hall or the summer outing to Roker and Seaburn. The Scouts met in a tumbledown and dusty premises in Elvet Waterside, near Peele's the vets. The entrance led upstairs to a large meeting room where formal ceremonies were held and games, such as British Bulldog, were played and the building had other holes and corners where patrol activity took place. In the summer there would be "wide" games in Little High and/or Houghall Woods. These usually took the form of an individual, or small group, laying a trail by hanging pieces of coloured wool or similar material from the vegetation. The rest of us would follow, with varying degrees of enthusiasm and sometimes getting sidetracked if we found something more interesting to do along the way.

When Skipper Morse was in charge his Lagonda was the 1st Durham (St Oswald's) troop transport. Our neckerchief colours were blue and gold and there'd often be heckling and joshing if our car encountered the 5th Durhams (palatinate purple and grey) and Skipper Dr Chalmers in his open Austin. There was a great and friendly rivalry between these groups.

When Skipper Morse moved to Carlisle the Rev. Kenneth Meux took over the parish but not the Scouts. Don Robson was the new GSM and under his direction gang shows, with the Guides involved as well, gave many of us our first experience of treading the boards. The choruses and sketches appeared to delight the audiences that packed the Institute. Riding along on the crest of a wave? We certainly were.

My only personal recollections of these were taking part in a sketch "The Colonel takes a bath" on one occasion and in a gymnastic display on another. But Dorothy Shea (now Summerbell) has kept the programmes and they confirm that not only was "The Colonel" a feature of the April 1950, show, there was also a sword-dancing item in which I think I would have taken part.

Furthermore, the January, 1949, programme places me in a sketch entitled "The Operation." This was a piece of mime in silhouette, backlit onto a white-sheet screen, in which a "patient" lay on a table while a "surgeon", using an outsize saw and knife, supported by his only-too-willing assistants, removed a large number of gruesome items from the poor chap's stomach, passed upwards by a boy hidden under the table. These included such things as a horse-shoe, alarm clock (which conveniently goes off) and finally, the pièce de resistance, a very long string of sausages.

RIGHT & INSET: In the days of few motor vehicles, the Vicar's Lagonda was a distinctive sight in Durham's streets in the 1940s. Here it is with a quartet of Scouts in the Lake District. Clockwise from back left: Mark Turner, Brian Shaw, Peter Cherry and Colin Shaw.

The first night the show went very much as expected with fairly enthusiastic applause but on the second night during the course of the "operation" we were mystified by the audience dissolving into gales of laughter and obviously finding it so much funnier than the previous night's. The answer was that the stage hands had forgotten to mask off the underside of the table and the audience not only saw the operation but also what they were not supposed to see – the enthusiastic efforts of the boy among the "entrails" beavering away under the table.

These cheerful productions typified the optimistic outlook of the post-war years and the sense of relief that, though it was difficult with shortages at times, life could slowly return to normal.

ABOVE: St Oswald's Youth Fellowship in the Vicarage garden, 1949, one a series of pictures taken for the Rev Hilary and Mrs Morse on their departure for a new parish in Carlisle. Back row (from left): Brian Shaw, David Young, ?, Terence Coulson, John Coulson, Second row: Marjorie Smith, Audrey Caveney, Peter Mills, Colin Forrester, Derek Storey, David Milner, Gordon Alderson, ?, Jackie Greener, Elsie Loftus, Margaret Gustard. Seated: Stephanie Davis, Kathleen Surtees, Doreen Maddison, - Wood, June McIntyre, Mrs Morse, Dorothy Shea, Winifred Slater, Gladys Parlett, Audrey McIntyre. In front: Don Robson and Malcolm Willis.

LEFT: Scouts and Guides' guard-of-honour for the wedding of St Oswald's Vicar, the Rev. Hilary B. Morse and Miss Theresa Bolland in April 1944. Over the vicar's shoulder can be seen Dr Michael Ramsey, later to become Bishop of Durham and Archbishop of Canterbury. Also present were the Bishop of Durham, the Dean of Carlisle Cathedral and the Dean of York Minster.

BELOW: Gang show scene, from left: Gladys Parlett, John Lightfoot, Audrey McIntyre, Kenneth Hayton, Winifred Slater, Don Robson and Elsie Loftus.

ABOVE: *Gang show 1949. Second left of the Sea Rangers in the back row is Jean Urquhart, who died soon afterwards. The author is immediately in front of her – in a cast of almost ninety local kids.*

RIGHT (TOP): *Gang show 1950. Among those not included in other pictures are John Craggs (front left), Leslie Vayro (third left, second row), Frank Delap (second left, third row), Anthony Willis (fourth left, third row) and Heather Newsom (extreme right, third row).*

RIGHT (BOTTOM): *Visiting day to the Sea Rangers' camp of Grange-in-Borrowdale. Among the guests are, front left, Mrs Shea, of Highwood View. Next to her in light-coloured hat is Miss Tindale, of Hallgarth Street. On the extreme right are Mr and Mrs Billy McIntyre, of Mount Joy Crescent, and Mrs Stobbs, of Whinney Hill.*

Under the Rev Hilary Morse, the Vicarage was virtually open house to the people of the parish and the door was often left open for people to wander in. Groups of lads, particularly, could be found in a games room containing a billiards table, sets of chess and draughts and old copies of *Punch* magazine. The Vicarage was also the Sunday evening venue (after Evensong) of the Youth Fellowship and of the pre-Confirmation Catechism classes.

I attended these and I am indebted to Mary Almond for this extract from the December, 1948, edition of the parish magazine:

CONFIRMATION: *The following were confirmed by the Bishop of Jarrow, on December 1st, in St Oswald's Church:- Terence Coulson, Frank Delap, Joseph Eves, Tom Keegan, William Petrie, Clive Titman, Malcolm Willis,* **David Young**; *Mrs Casson, Mrs Parker, Mrs Shippen, Margaret Almond, Winona Barr, Kathleen Hogg, Heather Newson, Gladys Parlett, Ann Percy, Marie Petrie; and the following Bow School boys: Gordon Bell, Peter Farrage, Peter Hansen, Christopher Place, Malcolm Seed, Tony Sparrow, Peter Stimpson.*

The Youth Fellowship also met at the Institute, on Tuesday nights, I think. The fellowship's main activities were table tennis and barn dancing, with the Rev Kenneth Meux (a nice man but not the greatest swinger in town) presiding over the gramophone while the girls attempted to polish their fancy footwork by cajoling reluctant youths onto the floor for the Veleta or Gay Gordons or some Victor Silvester number. My two left feet were not

LEFT (TOP): Guides' farewell picture to Mrs Morse, 1949. Back row (from left): Dorothy Shea, Audrey Stobbs, Doreen Maddison, June McIntyre, Kathlen Surtees, Sheila Brown, Margaret Pawson, Jean Urquhart, Stephanie Davies, Elsa Bunting. Second row: Audrey McIntyre, Maureen Hogg. Moira Keegan, Eleanor Todd, ?, Pat Waites, ?, Ruby Spikings, Kathleen Hogg, Margaret Wales, Margaret Almond, ?. Third row: Ethel Dunn, Marie Petrie, Margaret Morris, Miss Gardiner, Mrs Morse, Freda Davies, Gladys Partlett, Anne Dods, Elsie Loftus, Aline Corner, Sheila Mitchinson, Tessa Rabole or Trish Melville, Winifred Slater. Front row: Jean Thompson, ?, Betty Loftus, ?, ?, Pat Lancaster, ?, ?, ?, ?, ?.

LEFT: St Oswald's Sunday School, June 1949, in St Chad's College grounds. From left (back), Malcolm Willis, Whinney Hill; Margaret Almond, Highwood View; Kathleen Hogg, Durham Police Station; Gordon Graham, St Oswald's curate; Jean Thompson, - Thompson; Billy Hugill, Highwood View; (front), Kenneth Hodgson and Sheila Hodgson, Hallgarth Street; Ann Slack, Whinney Hill; Ann Mitchell, Boyd Street; Maureen Hogg, Police Station; ?. Gordon Graham was an enthusiastic curate who quickly involved himself with the youth of the parish, as an ideal colleague for the Rev Kenneth Meux, a vicar of serious and more spiritual disposition.

among their prime targets and those of us who would sooner have been swallowed up by a hole in the ground than be seen dancing with girls drifted out into the street. Meanwhile, in the smaller meeting room just across the passage it was possibly not just coincidence that the middle-aged matrons of the parish, including stepmother Florrie, were playing their weekly whist, organised by Mrs Gilvey.

Before deserting the Scouts for the Air Training Corps (run for many years by Cecil Ferens, a leading City personality, solicitor and sportsman, with the help of Bill Harrison, a Johnston School history master), I enjoyed camping at Blanchland – and later learning Northumbrian sword dancing. Performed with great gusto and, perhaps, with less finesse by young Scouts than it should have been, this was a very acceptable alternative for boys who were, as yet, a little shy of sharing the floor with the girls.

We were taught the moves and practised with all the gracefulness we could muster by Don Robson and I believe Joe Bray. Among the team were possibly Peter Cherry from Houghall, John Lightfoot from Mount Joy Crescent, John Craggs, Colin Shaw, Anthony or Malcolm Willis, myself and one or two others. We started with wooden swords but when we became sufficiently accomplished some metal versions were produced for us.

The dances consisted of circles, lines, crossovers and stepovers in a variety of patterns with sword blades occasionally clashed to the beat of the traditional folk music. The dances culminated in the raising of the interlocked swords in an impressive star shape. These performances impressed people, so much so that Skipper Morse summoned us to his new parish in Carlisle to perform, maybe it was for his institution and induction. It was in an October half-term holiday that we set out on this adventure with Don Robson at the wheel of his (inevitably) open topped 1930s Morris Oxford.

He gave us an extended ride through the Cheviots to arrive at the new Morse vicarage in the evening. I suppose we were fed and then in due course billeted in various parts of the establishment.

John Craggs and I were allocated the caravan in the garden – bitterly cold and uncomfortable.

LEFT (TOP): Part of St Oswald's church choir of 1942. This group includes Jim Davies (front left), whose parents kept the Three Hearts of Gold inn just opposite the vestry. The cheery lad on the extreme right looks to me like Mac Forrester, of Hallgarth View, whose father had sadly died the previous year. He has his arm over the shoulder of Alan Shea, of Highwood View, and front right is Mac's brother Colin. Second left front looks like Billy Todd and the lad in the middle wearing glasses is John Crossland.

LEFT: St Oswald's Sunday School group out on a ramble with Gordon Graham. Back (from left), Ann Mitchell, Kathleen Hogg, Maureen Hogg; front, Edward Almond, Kathleen and Sheila Hodgson, Kenneth Hodgson.

But being resourceful scouts we did something we shouldn't have done – we lit the gas burners on the caravan cooker. It warmed us up a little but I think we sensed that it was dangerous and after a while we put out the gas. Next evening we were on parade for our grand performance. We were decked out in a costume of white shirts, grey flannels with coloured sashes and plimsolls. I guess we'd rehearsed and all seemed well set for a great show.

I trust it really was not as bad as I recall. I think we'd negotiated the first dance OK but there came a point in one intricate movement when someone lost his way. Such is the nature of this dancing, that when one is lost all are lost, and as uncoordinated bodies panicked and flew off in all directions the show ended in a total shambles. The kind audience still applauded. Maybe they thought we meant it – but we were horrified.

The journey back through the Lake District on the next glorious autumn day was something to look forward to but if our first night in the caravan was what we called chilly, the next was arctic. We spent it on the upper ledge of a barn lent by a kind farmer near Sedbergh. The dried bracken being stored for animals' winter bedding looked inviting but, despite our blankets and as much clothing as we could put on, comfort and sleep eluded us. We arrived home tired and weary from our spartan adventure and much appreciative of home comforts. Did we get a badge for country dancing?

* * *

Ann Mitchell (now Ann Shaw, of Lincoln) lived at 4 Boyd Street, and was daughter of Jack and Clara. Jack worked for Durham City Council at the Town Hall and was a champion bowls player, a member of the Dunelm Club on the Racecourse.

*Ann recalls that as a Whinney Hill schoolgirl she attended Youth Fellowship in St Oswald's Vicarage on Sunday evenings – but not every Sunday. While her parents believed that was where she was, Ann confesses that sometimes she went to meet friends at the ice rink instead. A much more exciting prospect. She writes: "**I remember you living in a shop in Hallgarth Street and people such as John Craggs, Colin Shaw, Pete Cherry, Ruby Spikings, Ann Slack etc. I also remember the dances we had at St Oswald's Institute (Mr and Mrs Bray used to give us dancing lessons). Maureen and Kathleen Hogg were two others around our age, Keith Smith another – he lived at Shincliffe."***

These were early teen days, around 1949-51, when we wandered around in groups. Ann told of one bonfire night when she was not going to be let out unless her parents knew who she was with (that's how it used to be). Apparently, the gang came to an arrangement that we would announce our arrival in Boyd Street by letting off a banger on the Mitchell windowsill. Needless to say Jack and Clara jumped out of their skins and were quickly on the doorstep, with Ann grinning behind their backs. To this day Ann blames me for the banger. What the outcome was is beyond my recall. Sometimes youthful exuberance defies logic, though. Why didn't we just knock at the door?

* * *

Everyone's Heroine

Jean Urquhart was a cheerful, attractive teenager whose life was short – but who won the hearts of everyone who knew her through the courageous way she faced up to illness and lived out her meagre quota of days as fully as she could. Completely lacking self-pity she was outgoing and gregarious, winning a wide circle of supportive friends while an enthusiastic member of St Oswald's youth organisations.

Jean's parents, from South Shields, kept the New Inn at Church Street Head where my father was a "regular" and, because of my mother's premature death in 1941, he took an anxious interest in Jean's progress and, no doubt, suspected what lay in store for her. My mother and Jean, especially, lived in that tantalising period before the control or cure of many illnesses, now no longer fatal, had been perfected. Had they survived only a few more years. . . .who knows?

At the time parents had much to worry about over the health of their children with

mumps, chickenpox, measles, diphtheria and scarlet fever still causing serious illness – sometimes claiming lives – and with poliomyelitis (polio) emerging as a new and crippling scourge.

ABOVE: Jean Urquhart's party, December 1946: From left (back row): Gordon Alderson, Jimmy Davies, Eddie –, Roger Lightfoot, Lilian Vest, Dorothy Shea, Margaret Pawson; (second row) Joan Barr, Sylvia Forbes, Stephanie Davies, Colin Forrester, Gerry Kelly, Kathleen Surtees, Pat Wood, Audrey Stobbs, ?, June McIntyre, Fred Smurthwaite and Neville Boyd; (seated), Marjorie Smith, Pam Oliver, Peter Mills, Billy Irving, Derek Storey, Jean Urquhart, Wesley Jackson, Jean's cousin, Audrey Caveney; (front), Alan Wiper, Ken Wills, Jack Greener and Ian Herbert.

LEFT: Jean Urquhart, of the New Inn, showing her Medal of Fortitude – dubbed the Guides' VC – for her brave fight against rheumatic fever to her Girl Guide colleagues. From left (front), Sheila Tate, Audrey Owens, Doreen Blackett, Winifred Slater, Audrey McIntyre, Dorothy Adair; (middle) Elsa Bunting, Pauline Lax, –, Stephanie Davies, Ethel Dunn; (back) Marjorie Smith, Pam Oliver, Freda Benson, Audrey Stobbs. Among those mostly hidden are Mrs Morse and Freda Davies.

Jean was only 19 when she died and a large contingent of young people from St Oswald's attended her funeral in her home town of South Shields, to which the family had returned. Young men from the parish were her bearers and, of course, the Guide movement was repre-sented in force. While she was a member of the St Oswald's com-pany, the Guides had honoured Jean in 1946 with their Medal of Fortitude in the presence of her Guiding friends who are unlikely ever to forget her.

Let the *Durham Advertiser* (May 17, 1946) tell her story:–

"Tonight the courage under prolonged suffering of Girl Guide Jean Urquhart, who at 16 has survived double pneumonia and four attacks of rheumatic fever, will be recognised at the weekly meeting of her troop, 6th Durham St Oswald's Company, when she will receive the Girl Guides' VC, the association's supreme and rarely bestowed honour. Jean is the only child of Mr Norman Urquhart, licensee of the New Inn, Durham, and Mrs Urquhart. Along with her medal, Jean will be presented with a citation which states that while in bed with rheumatic fever she had borne her pain with fortitude and without a word of complaint.

Mrs Morse, Guide Captain and wife of the Rev H.B. Morse, Vicar of St Oswald's, received the medal on Saturday and broke the news to Jean, who was so excited she forgot about her usual early bed time and made a late night of receiving the congratulations of her friends."

The *Advertiser* recounted that Jean had contracted double pneumonia, aged two, and rheumatic fever, aged four, which recurred at nine and 13, each illness lasting four months until her most recent attack from which she began recuperating a month ago. This kept her in bed for the better part of nine months.

Mrs Urquhart, who nursed her single-handedly, said that Jean had always been able to crack a joke, even when she was at her lowest, and always looked forward to the day when she would be well and able to go for walks. Jean has now realised that ambition and on Easter Sunday, her first outing, went to church to receive Communion.

During the Forties many children struggled through life with all sorts of physical impairments that can be cured today – various limps, cross-eyes, bowed legs, club feet, hare lips, cleft palates, hunched backs and so on. Sometimes bravery was simply the ability to put up with the affliction, count your blessings, and mix well with the more fortunate children – Jean did all of that but with the added virtue of being an inspirational, shining, and forever smiling example to all.

Chapter VI

OVER THE CEMETERY WALL

There were no public recreation areas for the children of Elvet that I can recall. The nearest swings and roundabouts were in Wharton Park, North Road, and they were always pretty ropy. We were, however, quite resourceful in finding our own play areas – Little High Wood, Palmer's Close for formal games such as cricket and football and, of course the streets themselves. Highwood View, being a cul-de-sac at least as far as heavy traffic was concerned, was a safe and popular place to play in the Forties, not surprisingly as a fair number of children lived there and in the nearby streets.

The largest family was the Owens. The eldest was Charles (known as Junior), a little older than us and not so evident as my contemporary Audrey, a lively girl and a natural leader, who later worked for some years at the Palladium cinema in Claypath. Only a little younger was Betty, then came Barry and later another sister Valerie. So for quite a while there was usually an Owens to be seen in the street.

Activities were the usual chasing and hiding games, riding bikes and trikes, plus tennis-ball games such as football, cricket and french cricket. Hopscotch was popular with the girls and was marked out on the road or footpath with chalk, or with a piece of slate or soft stone. Most of the activity centred on the area around the Owens' home at No 8 and the gable end of No 15 on the opposite corner. This was the home of Leslie Vayro, and younger sister Christine, whose parents were extremely tolerant of us marking a goal or wicket on the wall and of the consequent thumping of a ball against it. Leslie's father Cyril Vayro used to cycle to work at the vehicle licensing office at Elvet station and was one of the first in the street to buy a car after the war, a Ford Eight, which he kept in a garage next to the New Inn in Church Street Head. Leslie himself suffered from asthma, an affliction apparently less common among children then than it is now, and it was quite frightening when he had an attack. The last I heard of him was when he was a pathology lab assistant at Bishop Auckland Hospital in the late Fifties. His father died quite young.

Another favoured play area was the cemetery wall at the back of John Craggs' home in Gladstone Villas in the lane that led into the back of Boyd Street, near Mr Heckles' garden (now occupied by garages). The stone wall, with round-topped coping stones, was low on the lane side and high on the cemetery side. It was convenient to sit astride and much time was spent "hanging around" there.

In the cemetery there were bushes ideal for hiding games but returning to the lane required some climbing effort. At some points the wall was clad with orange-flowered nasturtiums and ivy, which helped, but scrabbling for a foothold sometimes meant the toes of your shoes became seriously scuffed (trouble when you got home). Usually to be found there would be John Craggs, Leslie Vayro, Kathleen and Maureen Hogg, Paul Allison, Margaret and Edward Almond, some of the Owens clan and maybe from time to time Ann Mitchell from Boyd Street, Pat Waites from Anchorage Terrace, John and Clive Titman from Highwood Terrace and Ian and Sheila Mitchinson from Union Place.

The permutations varied over the years as people came and went. The Hogg girls, for example, were daughters of a police sergeant who rose rapidly in the ranks to become Deputy Chief Constable and, after leaving 13 Highwood View, they lived for a long time in the police station house in Court Lane. Replacing them in Highwood View was another police family, the Hugills, whose son Billy became part of the gang.

The Titman family moved into the house we vacated in Highwood Terrace on moving to Hallgarth Street. Their father was from the Peterborough area and their mother, a skilled needlewoman, was well known by her maiden name Flossie Hindle. The lads were good pals, renowned as being brighter than average at school, and it was on their bikes I learnt to ride two-wheelers. The Almond family was well-established in Highwood View, running a plumbing and heating business from a yard behind the houses. Grandfather Edward lived at No. 10 and Arthur, his wife Phyllis (née Derry) and children at No. 1. Their handcart was a familiar scene around the streets but it was later replaced by an Austin van, which was hand-painted by my father. The family all worshipped at St Oswald's and for a while Arthur was a churchwarden. Daughter Margaret (now at Carlisle) is roughly my age and I recall birthday parties for her at No. 1. Edward, who now runs the business is a few years younger and youngest of all is Mary, a post-war baby, now a schoolteacher at Fishburn, who lives in her grandparents' old house at No. 10 – representing roughly the whole of the 20th Century in Highwood View.

Mary is the family archivist and has researched the

ABOVE LEFT & LEFT: Mr and Mrs Edward Almond, outside their home 10 Highwood View. A quiet backwater devoid of vehicles then. Contrast today, cars parked at every door.

business back to its foundation in 1848. "Robert Robson Almond (of Church Street) was the founder of the business," she writes. "It then passed to his son Nicholas Watson Almond (my great grandfather), then Edward (my grandfather), then Arthur (my father) and finally to Edward (my brother).

"Nicholas Watson Almond died, aged 78, in July, 1923. The newspaper account of his death says he was apprenticed to his father as a plumber and later carried on as a master plumber for 40 years. He must have retired in 1911 – 12 years before his death. He lived at 1 Highwood View when he died."

The Craggs family in Gladstone Villas were also devout churchpeople. John's grandfather, Mr Chapman, a neat little chap with a goatee beard, was a staunch Methodist and a lay preacher, I believe, with Shincliffe connections, who spent

BELOW (LEFT): Proud Guides, Sheila Mitchinson, of Union Place (left) and Margaret Almond, outside Margaret's back gate in Highwood View.

BELOW (RIGHT): Dorothy Shea (left) escorts new girl Margaret Almond from Highwood View to her first day at Durham Girls' Grammar School in September, 1946. Would Church Street Head be so quiet at 8.30am today?

hours at his Bible. He was also a skilled colourist using pastels to bring to life black and white photographs.

By contrast John's parents attended St Nicholas' Church in the Market Place. His father, a little older than the average parent, worked at the Dean and Chapter office and dressed the part in pinstriped trousers and black jacket. He also kept an immaculate allotment at the top of the Banks, down the track leading from Quarry Heads Lane. John was musically gifted and was a friend in the Scouts and Air Training Corps.

There is a danger of creating the impression that we were all little angels playing in an idyllic setting but it is true to say that some Highwood View residents did get upset if the noise was too much and if the odd window got broken. And we were not above pranks, like tying neighbouring door knobs together, knocking at the doors and running away.

There was certainly no wilful damage committed for the fun of it, nor did old folk live in fear of the youth of the day, nor was there any question of serious defiance of adult authority. But there's no doubt we could at times be a nuisance – and cheeky with it – and the older generation could and did chastise us without fear of reprisal from our parents. In everyday matters, adults were something like an informal grand alliance and, usually, if it became known that you'd been in trouble with one of them you were in trouble with your parents too. As confidence grew, we spread our wings and wandered farther afield. A favourite ramble or bike ride saw us ascend South Road, past the Golf Club to the Cock o' the North at Farewell Hall and return via the A1 (which actually had a cycle track alongside for about half a mile) to Merry Oaks and the Duke of Wellington, descending Potters Bank to Quarry Heads Lane, thence to the New Inn. This could be varied by cutting across to the A1, via Clarty Lonnen, from the Golf Club or by turning into Elvet Hill Road (round the Peacocks, as we called it) and taking Green Lane to Merry Oaks.

There was little danger to us from traffic but parents warned us loud and long to keep away from the river, unless we were being taken on a formal walk. But, of course, we were occasionally tempted and it is with some horror now that I remember playing on the steep rocky banks, near the Cat's Well below St Oswald's Church, where there's quite a precipitous descent to the river – a river that was then heavily polluted, flowing almost black, and supporting little life other than slimy leeches. The Wear's life seems to have returned to something like it was in my dad's youth at the beginning of the 1900s. He used to talk of seeing salmon leaping the weirs near Prebends Bridge and at Framwelgate.

We would also spend hours, particularly during the school holidays, in Little High Wood, taking a bottle of pop, or even water, to sustain us. The Hollow, now pretty well overgrown, was a sandy area with convenient tree stumps to serve as a wicket for cricket, a base for rounders, or goalposts for football. It was used for picnics and also on summer evenings for formal gatherings of Scouts, Guides, Cubs or Brownies. Sadly, the wood today appears to be little used but in the Forties it was an adventure playground for carefree children. Incidental attractions were the underground shelters at the foot of the wood and the trenches, dug by the military early in the war, either for training or as defensive measures when invasion threatened.

These were little used for the purposes intended; the shelters soon became a bit rank but the trenches particularly were pressed into service by lads as part of their own war games. Entering the wood from the Mount Joy end meant crossing the little stream that was later piped and here we would also mess about, making dams so that the stream deepened and backed up. If we did not release the flood before we left, gardeners in the Klondike allotments would get angry because their water supply had dried up.

Most play in the wood was a summer activity but the place came to life in spring when the woodland floor was carpeted with bluebells. But not for long. These colourful flowers attracted children, particularly girls, and the blooms were carried home by the armful to decorate the home. A bunch of bluebells in a jam jar, for a few days at least, brightened many a kitchen window sill. No one gave it a second thought. Environment and ecology were words unheard of. Have the bluebells actually faded away? I hope not.

While summer had its obvious attractions for kids whose time was spent largely outdoors, winter brought its special pleasures. Snow was expected after Christmas and more or less arrived on cue in January and February, bringing unalloyed pleasure and excitement to children and dismay to adults, who in the case of prolonged or heavy snow and frost, had much to cope with.

For them it was a case of "life goes on". They struggled to work if they could and were not browbeaten into staying at home by local radio producing minute -by-minute accounts of trouble here, there and everywhere. If conditions were too severe to get about work began at once to remedy the situation. An army of householders and shop workers immediately set about clearing their own frontages, making it possible, at least, to move about the streets. It was not uncommon to see snow piled a couple of feet high in the gutter but the irony was when the snowplough came round to clear the road it was all thrown back on to the footpath again.

In freezing weather the main problem facing besieged householders with outside toilets was frozen pipes. Smelly little oil lamps were placed in the toilet overnight to take the edge off the frost and the plumbers made a fortune when the thaw came.

It was the season of chilly bedrooms with lino on the floor which was so icy cold it had you hopping about until you got your socks on. You could see your breath on the air and miraculous frost patterns on the window panes. But a hot water bottle and dad's heavy NFS greatcoat thrown over the bed when he arrived home had helped to ward off the worst Jack Frost could do during the night.

Waking up to an unusual but distinctive lightness and the hush of a muffled dawn might be the first hint that the snow had arrived. Word might get round that school was closed, as it was in 1947, and if so it was hotfoot to Mount Joy Hill with sledge in tow. Dozens of people would assemble there and a track would soon be established. The more ambitious would head off to Observatory Hill by the side of Potters Bank – a longer and faster track. Here injuries were not uncommon, and one year Paul Allison broke his skull crashing into a tree and was rushed to hospital for a major operation. He recovered OK, though his head was swathed in bandages for quite a while. I sometimes wondered whether the crack I'd administered with a toy mallet some years earlier might have left a weakness.

An impromptu sledging track from the back of Hallgarth View on Whinney Hill, down towards Hallgarth Farm was a favourite with youngsters from Hallgarth Street but often ruined by responsible, but to us, inconsiderate adults putting ashes on the glacial surface so they could walk safely. Spoilsports!

Sliding was another form of winter entertainment, though tough on the footwear. A good long slide was often produced on the land in Church Street Head next to St Oswald's school yard. If you got your run up right you could glide, arms akimbo, for 25 yards or more. But if a bare patch appeared in the ice and you caught it, the fun was brought to an abrupt and painful end.

Skating was not on the agenda, except at the ice rink, but it had been a feature of Durham winters in years gone by. People inevitably reminisce about big freeze-ups and Dad was no exception, claiming to recall one winter when there was an ox-roast on the river. The book *Durham – Cathedral City* contains a picture of skating near Prebend's Bridge when the river froze over for several weeks. That was in 1895, eight years before Dad was born, so it was possibly just a tale handed down by his parents.

We remember the fun and excitement but what about the pain? Chapped hands aching in the cold, frozen feet smitten with chilblains, and bare legs chafed raw by welly tops. Out came the block of Snowfire ointment at bed time to soothe the sores, ready for the fray next day – until the thaw reduced the winter wonderland to a miserable dark brown slush. Could spring be far behind?

Games in street and schoolyard were played according to season – conkers being the obvious example of an autumn game, though a wrinkled old horse chestnut could linger in a boy's trouser pocket, along with bits of string, old acorns, a few marbles and a pen-knife for months on end.

A decent stick, to use as a sword perhaps, and home-made catapults and bows and arrows were among a lad's armoury in the woods, though it should be said that most were used for games only and were hardly effective enough to inflict any serious damage. The stick, of course, was also used to poke any apparently inanimate object of dubious identity to see if would spring into life or to check whether it was safe to pick it up. You knew you had a very good stick indeed if an adult admonished you with the oft-heard "You'll put someone's eye out with that."

The era of Richmal Crompton's William and his gang was still lingering on, though I would guess the wartime generation was the last to play Marbles and Five Stones (chucks) seriously. One game that did appear to flourish as a result of wartime shortages was Spanners. Cigarette cards had ceased to be issued but many remained on the scene, and those that were not part of serious collections were folded over one another to form a square shape, their adhesive backs being used to hold them together to make what was called a spanner. The first player flicked a spanner from between forefinger and thumb (the hand being held palm upwards) and the second player did likewise, attempting to get his spanner as near to the first as possible. If he could span the distance between the two with thumb and little finger he won his opponent's spanner – and so the game went on in turns. In suitable weather at playtime several groups of lads would amuse themselves with these games – but in the evening and at holiday times informal games of football or cricket, with goals or wickets chalked onto the boys' toilets wall, were played in St Oswald's School yard. There was the occasional broken window and frequent shinning up drainpipes to recover balls from the guttering. In cricket a one-hand catch off roof or wall was "out." But we had to take flight if the caretaker hove into view.

* * *

It was little wonder parents had a horror of children playing near the river because it was it always regarded as treacherous. Nevertheless pleasure boating, as well as the sport of rowing, has proved a popular pastime in the City. The most notable river

tragedy of the Forties, which attracted widespread interest, occurred in April 1947, when two young men from outlying villages went over the Museum Dam, downstream from Prebend's Bridge, in their pleasure boat. The loss of two young lives was shocking enough in itself but their families' grief was intensified by the fact that, despite the river being searched by police with grappling hooks, the bodies were not recovered for about two weeks. I happened to be at the Millburngate Waterside (one Saturday morning, I think), when the body of one of the unfortunates, bloated and terribly discoloured, was hauled ashore through the railings near the old nursery school. A grim reminder, indeed, of the risk of ignoring the warning that used to be clearly displayed on its buttresses of the danger of boating beyond Prebend's Bridge.

ALLOTMENTS

A family's Mount Joy legacy

In the Dig for Victory years for the Second World War, growing vegetables on local allotments was an important and, no doubt rewarding activity. As well as the large area given over to these plots in Stockton Road, there were also allotments in School Lane, near the Banks off Quarry Heads Lane, and in South Road, near the entrance to Little High Wood. Jenifer Blair, of Back Mount Joy, who was born in 1942, recalls this keenness for gardening. "My main recollections from my childhood are of the number of allotments in the area, where I would be sent out to see if anyone had any spare veg for our Sunday lunch.

"I also remember taking our golden labrador for walks through Little High Wood and High Wood. Up Hollingside Lane to the old golf course was another favourite route."

Jenifer is the daughter of Gladys Blair (neé Coates), a member of the Coates building firm that was prominent in the life of St Oswald's church and the community. It was Jenifer's great grandfather Thomas Coates, who at the turn of the 19th/20th Century demolished the Racecourse grandstand and used the stone for the impressive frontages of the houses in Mount Joy Crescent. (My parents spent the last days of their lives

BELOW: Jenifer Blair - a Forties snap in the Garden of the family home in Mount Joy Crescent

 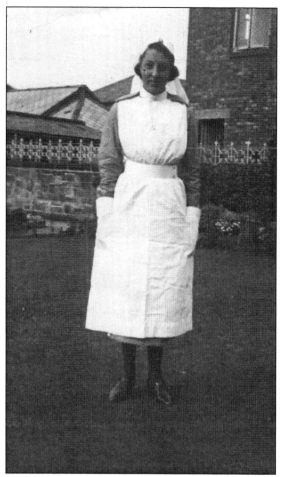

ABOVE (LEFT): Portrait of a Back Mount Joy family, the Slaters, the little girl is now a grandmother, Win Coleman.

ABOVE (RIGHT): Gladys Coates, Jenifer's mother, who ran the Durham School of Dancing, pictured in wartime VAD uniform. The railings on top of the wall behind her were removed for the war effort.

at No 5 and my Aunt Meg and Uncle Tom Broughton lived at No 7 for a while in the late Sixties and early Seventies).

Girls particularly will remember the Durham School of Dancing at Mount Joy which Gladys Coates ran from 1935 to 1996, latterly with Jenifer's help. In the 1930s, Coates built the terrace of cottages in Back Mount Joy, where my Aunt Olive and Uncle Ted White lived for many years, and also where Winifred Slater (now Win Colman), who has been a tower of strength collecting pictures and information for this work, lived with her parents. What used to be Coates' builder's yard, entered from the top of Hallgarth Street, is now the site of Hallgarth Nursing Home.

Chapter VII

PLAYING WITH FIRE

What was Hallgarth Street like in the 1940s? In appearance little different from today, though much less "gentrified." Its variety of houses ranged from the grand and elegant to the tumbledown near-slum. At the Elvet end in particular there were gaps where houses had either been pulled down or, judging by the remaining ruins, had fallen down. Elvet House stands on one of these sites today.

Most of the houses were well maintained but a significant number were somewhat shabby, perhaps reflecting the poverty of the tenants. Few people in the street possessed cars so there was not the parking blight so evident today, but it was nevertheless a busy traffic route in and out of town. More people walked and it was not uncommon for people on their way to and from Houghall or Shincliffe to call into our shop, particularly the Land Army girls.

It was an outward route for Trimdon Motor Services (TMS) buses which departed from Old Elvet for East Durham pit villages. "Tommy's Mucky Shirts" or "Trimdon Muck Shifters" we used to call them. The old fleet of pre-war Dennis buses laboured up Elvet bank, and as they arrived on the level in Hallgarth Street began moving up the gears to pick up speed, belching out thick black exhaust clouds across the pavement. Not very healthy but we thought little of it.

The United town service bus also ran through the street every 25 past and five to the hour. In the post-war years this bus was easy to pick out because it was different from United's fleet of Bristols, being a smaller Albion if I remember rightly. There were two bus stops for the town service – one at the Elvet end at Woodcocks (the grocery shop where, apparently, my Aunt Olive worked as a girl in the early part of the century) and one at Mount Joy.

Generally the residents swept and swilled their own frontages and whitened their front steps with a chalky stone but every now and then a load of coal would be delivered unbagged into the gutter. The recipient would either carry it into the house, bucket by bucket, or shovel it into the cellar, carefully leaving behind a small pile of unwanted grey slag for the road sweeper to take away in his barrow.

There were three pubs: the Spread Eagle at the Elvet end, the Sun halfway up the east side and the Victoria at the foot of Church Lane on the other side, right opposite our shop. The busy Victoria was run by Mr and Mrs Petrie, whose son Bill and daughter Marie were slightly older contemporaries of mine, but part of the wartime generation of playmates brought up in the neighbourhood. This was a different environment from Highwood View, though only a few hundred yards away. Our playground here was not so much the street itself as what we called "the old buildings" – the ruins of old houses which were an adventure playground long before the modern concept was thought of. The land behind them stretched to the prison wall and was bounded on the south side by the back lane of Mavin Street and on the north by Palmer's Garth, which included a development of modern semis accessed from Elvet Crescent.

BELOW: All set for an outing from the Victoria Inn in Hallgarth Street. The group includes Harry Usher, Jim Davies (at back, wearing trilby), landlord Jimmy Reynolds (in shirtsleeves), Fred Benson (in dark trilby) and Jimmy Oliver (right).

Here we literally played with fire: clay puffers, which as their name suggests were small square-shaped vessels moulded out of clay with a ventilation hole in each side. They were filled with decayed wood, touch wood, which after being lit would eventually glow in the draught created as one ran along. An alternative was the fire-can – usually a pierced baked bean tin filled with combustible contents, lit, and swirled round the head on the end of a long wire. In a very short time indeed the tin would glow red hot. The holes in the tin would be made with a jack-knife, which many lads possessed in those days.

Other hazardous playthings included old airguns, catapults and any decent stick you could lay your hands on. Stone fights on the old buildings were not uncommon. There was after all plenty of raw material to hand and it's amazing that no one was seriously hurt, considering the gusto with which we entered into these things.

For a diversion you could climb the brick wall into Palmer's Garth where there was a small army depot and play on the bren-gun carriers and lorries parked there. Overlooking the whole scene was the gaunt grey wall and small cell windows of the prison. To relieve their boredom, no doubt, prisoners would "signal" to us with flashing mirrors and we

BELOW: Stepmother Florrie (centre) on an outing with friends, possibly taking a well-earned day off from shop duties. Who are the others? I recognise some of the faces but cannot recall their names.

would return the compliment, as best we could, with pieces of broken glass glinting in the sun. Prisoners in their grey uniforms were occasionally encountered in the street as a working party with a handcart and accompanied by two or three prison officers, men of military bearing, tall and ramrod straight like Guardsmen. More benign entertainment was running around with a hoop or "booler" – preferably an old car tyre propelled and steered with a short stick. Failing that an old bike tyre or wheel or beer barrel hoop would do. Occasionally we would come across an old metal version, possibly manufactured as a toy in Victorian times. This was less fun though, for to prevent it from running away the handle was looped around the rim.

The old buildings were also scenes of celebration at the end of the war when bonfires were lit and fireworks, which most children had never witnessed in their lives before, were set off to the delight of all. Guy Fawkes night celebrations also resumed – an event we had not hitherto enjoyed.

Of course, girls did not take part in some of the rougher activities but the ones I remember from my Hallgarth Street childhood include Marie Petrie, Gladys Parlett, Joan Heron, Cynthia Livingstone, Ethel Dunn, Alice Patterson and Ruby Spikings (Palmer's Garth). Among the lads were Billy

TOP RIGHT & RIGHT: Two faces of me. One taken on the back wall in Mavin Street (behind the Hallgarth Street shop), the other in South Road.

75

Tait, Billy Petrie, Billy Cauwood, Brian Wilson, Derek Hudspeth, Kenneth Hodgson; Kenneth Macdonald (Mavin Street); Eric Robinson (Church Lane); Ernie Benson (High Yard); Malcolm Ogden, Frank Lincoln and Trevor Elliot (Elvet Crescent) and Tommy Hazelgreaves (New Elvet).

Children usually stuck to their own patch and formed gangs but because I had already made friends there I wandered backwards and forwards between Hallgarth Street and Highwood View. The kids from the latter would never have ventured to the "old buildings", but the Hallgarth Street gang would sometimes range as far as Little High Wood or to the field at Palmer's Close, Church Street Head, to play football, or cricket.

Through my shop duties as an errand boy, delivering bread in a basket over my arm, I became quite well known in Whinney Hill. My route took me through The Hallgarth, by the ancient tithe barn, which was the prison officers' club house. There were also Bond's the joiners and undertakers, whose family lived in Hallgarth Street and, more importantly to children, Broughton's (later Fentiman's) pop factory, grandly called Prospect Works. My aunt Meg married into the Broughton family and Mrs Broughton (née Fentiman) also lived in Hallgarth Street. Seeing hundreds of bottles coming off a conveyor having been filled and sealed ready for crating seemed a miracle of automation at the time, though by then the machinery was probably quite old. Dandelion and Burdock, Cherryade and Cream Soda were favourites but the factory was renowned for its Hop-ade, with a beery flavour made from spent hops, and ginger beer, both of which were retailed in screw-top stone jars which kept the contents remarkably cool in those pre-refrigerator summers.

A chap called Arthur Pattison, who wore a brown overall, was a familiar figure there as was, after the war, George Craggs who had been a Far East PoW. Fentimans, who were based at Gateshead, also had a depot on Teesside and George drove lorry and trailer to and fro with supplies and empties.

Through Kingston's farmyard and past the farmhouse on the opposite side of the Hallgarth there were other tracks up to Whinney Hill (by the boys' entrance to the school) and to Hallgarth View (a cul-de-sac off Whinney Hill) and from the latter track you could also double back into Hallgarth Street through a derelict gap next to the Sun Inn. That was an alternative route if the geese in the farmyard were looking aggressive.

I delivered to a number of houses in that area: Mrs Forrester (mother of Mac, Colin and Ann) and Mrs Stobbs (mother of Audrey) and Mrs Forrest, who my stepmother said, always wore black because she lost her husband in the first war and her son in the second. At the top of The Hallgarth, opposite the Whinney Hill bus stop, lived my father's Aunt Edie at No. 3, whose husband Fred Young had been a liveried coachman at the turn of the century. And beside the bus stop lived Aunt Bella, at No. 76, whose husband Charles Young was also my grandfather's brother. They had two daughters: Frances, who married late and went to live in West Wales, and Gladys, whose two daughters Ann and Wendy Stevenson continue to live in Highwood Terrace.

Sweets were the only item among the many commodities rationed during the war that children regarded as important. I was in a slightly privileged position when we lived in the Hallgarth Street shop – but even then the coupons returned to the authorities had to match up to the sweets bought from the wholesaler and sold to the public, so there was only little scope for extra treats.

However Ethel Pickering (née Dunn), whose father died when she was ten, fondly remembers my dad

ABOVE: Ann Stevenson, a half cousin, who has recently retired from teaching at Bowburn. Ann and sister Wendy, who works at the Cathedral Library, have lived in Highwood Terrace virtually all their lives.

because he quietly used to slip her a few sweets on the sly when she came into the shop. As kids we made imaginative use of off-ration commodities. It wasn't unusual to see us with yellow-stained mouths chewing a stick of licquorice root, sucking Rennies or any other non-prescription medicinal items available from Masons the Chemists in Saddler Street for coughs and bad throats.

Particularly popular were Victory V lozenges, shaped like a small brown tile and with a distinctively tangy flavour. They were very more-ish. I don't know whether it was true at that time, but they were said once to have contained a touch of laudanum or morphine or some other addictive opiate which made them very popular with old ladies. A safer bet were dried locust beans, imported from goodness knows where, which were shaped like a small flattened banana with a hard brown exterior and a sweet sugary texture. Another unlikely delicacy were cinnamon sticks, with their exotic spicy flavour. Maybe less well known, however, is that hidden from public view in Hallgarth Street's "old buildings" the more advanced young lads smoked them!

This somewhat eclectic diet was supplemented with fruit both legitimately and illegally obtained. The raiding of apple and pear trees was commonplace – usually before the fruits were fully ripe. Was the tummy ache really worth it? Then there were seasonal sticks of rhubarb, carrots, peas and beans occasionally plundered from allotments. All in all, a healthy intake.

*   *   *

In the latter half of the 20th Century Hallgarth Street produced two newspaper editors – myself and Michael Sharman. I took the orthodox route into local newspaper journalism, leaving the Johnston School at the age of 17 in January, 1953, with a princely five O-levels and joining the Durham County Advertiser, then a major influence on the city's affairs, under the editorship of Frank Rushford. A period of probation and nurturing under the Westminster Press's still-infant training scheme and service in the Advertiser series' Durham and Bishop Auckland offices was followed by RAF National Service in Singapore. My return in late 1958 virtually coincided with "Old Rush's" retirement and under new editor Fred Hurrell I became a sub-editor and sports editor, succeeding "Young Rush" (editor's son Frank Rushford Jr, who took a senior post with the Kent and Sussex Courier at Tunbridge Wells). I left for the Peterborough Evening Telegraph in 1960 and ten years later became editor of the Lincolnshire Free Press and Spalding Guardian, and then in 1984 editor-in-chief of the Lynn News and Advertiser and Norfolk Citizen, retiring in 1999.

Michael, whose family lived in a large house on the corner of The Hallgarth, went to Durham School and Cambridge, joining The Journal at Newcastle, where he became Industrial Correspondent. He later took up the editorship of the weekly Hexham Courant and died in harness in tragic circumstances in the 80s. Michael's father was a top man in the Provincial Laundry in Providence Row and at Sunderland and the family were regulars at Roker Park. Michael himself, an asthma sufferer, was a keen follower of Durham City RFC where he was a contemporary of the England star and city estate agent Mike Weston.

Chapter VIII

TROUNCED BY THE TOFFS

Palmer's Close playing field, near the New Inn traffic lights, is where local lads used to assemble for a game of cricket or football. I think it belonged to the Dean and Chapter and was officially for the Choristers' School, though to their credit we were never prevented from playing there.

Once, a group of us, possibly the Scouts, was unwise enough to challenge Bow School to a game of cricket. As a thriving prep school it had all the facilities – a nice picturesque playing field in Quarry Heads Lane, more or less opposite Palmer's Close, with sight screens and a properly prepared square. These boys had proper gear, whites etc.

By contrast, we paced out a pitch as best we could on the levellest bit of Palmer's Close. We had two or three pairs of tatty pads, four stumps (three for the batting end and one for the bowling) and any old bats we could muster. Our technique consisted of hurling the ball as hard as we could to the batsman, who in turn, would simply attempt to slog it as far as possible. If it cleared the field into the Banks it was a six. There were never enough of us to muster proper teams and none of us had proper coaching. Often, a lost ball – or the boy who owned the bat being called home at bedtime – brought the game to a premature conclusion.

Needless to say our challenge proved ill-advised. Bow School was, after all, coached by C.L. (Charlie) Adamson, a formidable City and County player in his day. We were unused to the game's formalities and subtleties, lacked talent and technique, and scored very few runs indeed. It was not so much the crack of leather against willow as leather against stumps. Like all good schoolboy stories of the day, it ended with

RIGHT: This view of the New Inn, taken from a crane building the new university science block in the late 1960s shows one of our favourite play areas of the Forties and early Fifties, Palmer's Close. It was not a rugby field then but our venue for informal games of football and cricket.

the prep school seeing off the townie challengers. So far as I can recall locals who went on to make names for themselves with the City cricket club included George Delap (who with his elder brother Frank from the prison officers' quarters on Whinney Hill was in the Scouts) and Roger Lightfoot, from Mount Joy, who was a little older than our circle.

Two of the area's outstanding personalities lived on the Church Street Head frontage of Palmer's Close. J.O.K. (Oliver) May, a first world war veteran, singer, music teacher, Cathedral lay clerk and St Oswald's sometime choirmaster, and J. Wesley Lisle. Mr Lisle was a deaf-mute cobbler with a little hut down by the side of his bungalow. He and his wife (who may have been deaf and dumb, too) had two daughters, Margaret and Ruth, who would help with the transactions if necessary. As with many cobblers, your shoes would be not quite ready when you called but Wesley would finish the job while you waited. What he did not appreciate was the tremendous din his machinery made in the tiny hut as he shaped and buffed the soles and heels and occasionally sent sparks flying as

the emery wheel fouled a metal heel plate. He was oblivious to it, of course. To a youngster, it was all a bit like Dante's Inferno.

Dad often told a tale against Wesley about a prisoner who had left some shoes to be repaired before he had been caught and sentenced. After two years inside, he was let out of Durham Jail, made his way up Church Street, and called into Wesley's asking for his shoes, obviously expecting them to be ready. As was his wont, Wesley picked over the huge pile of assorted boots and shoes on his bench then scribbled on a scrap of paper: "Call back next week." Actually, only our "best" shoes went to Wesley to be repaired. Dad possessed a last and during the war, particularly, he would mend our workaday boots and shoes with any bits of leather or rubber he could lay his hands on. Many a time while galloping along I would be stopped agonisingly in my tracks by a tack coming through the sole of my boot and piercing my foot.

* * *

L.H. (Len) Weight, popular "mine host" at the New Inn in the late Forties and early Fifties, had been a talented cricketer in his younger days. He played 68 matches for Durham County between 1913 and 1927, his highest score being 123 and his best bowling performance seven wickets for 65. He took seven West Indies wickets for 92 in a match at Feethams, Darlington, in 1923. At club level, Weight played for South Shields, the home of Westoe Brewery, who were owners of the New Inn.

From 1926 to 1945 C.L. (Charlie) Adamson, of Bow School, South Road, also played for the county in a total of 111 matches. An opening batsman his highest knock was 137 not out. In addition to coaching scores of youngsters, Adamson also opened the batting for the City club for many years with H.C (Cecil) Ferens. In the Forties, John Coates, of the Mount Joy building firm, and Jack Spikings, of Palmer's Garth, a Whinney Hill schoolmaster, also turned out for City.

* * *

I have some difficulty in accurately visualising the architecture of New Elvet as it used to be. Just after the war and through the Fifties it was a fascinating kaleidoscope of houses, pubs, shops and businesses, particularly its western side with premises backing on to the river. Descending steeply from Church Street it was always bustling with traffic and pedestrians making their way to and from town. There was no Kingsgate bridge; it was quite scruffy but there was a small group of council houses called Hatfield View, built only in the late twenties or early thirties at the foot of the steepest part of the bank, the demolition of which was, I thought at the time, something of a scandal; there was as yet no university development. There were many properties which were clearly slums and past redemption and it was "very Durham" – now it's more like a highway than a street.

That's nostalgia for you. We may regret the passing of time but I imagine few will really regret the sweeping away of the decayed parts of the city and surely welcome its sensitively accomplished transformation over the years. I write from exile in Norfolk and people from these parts who visit Durham, and know it's my home town, invariably comment on how impressive the city is.

The *Advertiser* ran a very effective campaign in the immediate post-war years, carrying a picture every week of the derelict, ugly, neglected parts of the city – there were many – and commenting on the contrast between the grandeur of its historic buildings and architecture and the terrrible eyesores of its workaday streets.

So, a walk down one of these streets, New Elvet, as it used to be. One of its distinctive features was a lamp standard in the middle of the road at the Hallgarth Street-Church Street fork. There was a gap, as a result of demolition, between the last house in Church Street and Sayles fish and chip shop, which was a magnet for youngsters who would gather there on Friday evenings after scouts and guides. A rudimentary garden was created by the City council in the gap and a path led to a viewpoint overlooking the river, the Cathedral towering over the whole scene. Now it's the approach to Kingsgate bridge.

Sayles was No. 46, Smurthwaite's shop at No. 49 sold odds and ends like needles, pins and shoelaces, etc and, I believe, was later occupied by Thew's, the fruit and veg retailer. At 54 there was the somewhat scruffy Hare and Hounds pub and, through the archway Jopling's, the joiners. A little farther down came the considerable business of Matthew Fowler, with its Alladin's-cave auction salerooms and removal vans.

The entrance to Hatfield View was more or less opposite Court Lane and the businesses resumed with electrical engineers C. Horne and Co. In summer its doors were often left ajar giving a fascinating glimpse of work going on, largely rewinding electric motors. Then came most tantalising of all for kids, Adams Dee Cee toffee factory with its sweet smells and girls in sticky overalls standing outside, favouring young passers-by with the occasional contraband sweet.

A contrasting odour of petrol and motor oils issued from Fowler and Armstrong's garage at the foot of the hill, then came more old dwellings with passages, Austin's antique shop (we called it a junk shop) and a sweet shop run by an old lady called Ginny Wilson.

A bus stop stood next to the old-established motor firm McIntyres, (now Embleton's) which had a showroom, petrol pumps and repair shop running down to the river before we arrive at Heslop's, the butchers (now Prontaprint), with its old slaughterhouse behind, the City Hotel and the Half Moon inn at the corner of Elvet Bridge. Occasionally, you would see cattle being delivered to meet their doom or encounter open cellar flaps as drays rolled off barrels of beer for the pubs.

The Three Tuns Hotel takes up most of the frontage on the opposite side of lower New Elvet but Rutherford's, the newsagent, on the corner of Old Elvet was where we got our *Beano* , *Dandy* and, later, *Eagle* comics. Nearby at No. 3 New Elvet the City Fish and Game Co (also known as Hedley's?) was the area's wet fish shop.

Up from the Three Tuns, Thompson's Red Stamp stores (grocers) had quite large premises and then there were offices (at some time the National Health prescriptions pricing bureau) to the corner of Court Lane. The remainder of the east side has changed little in appearance with its block of thirties-style shops set back from the road.

Among the businesses were Clarke's lending library, a tobacconist, a Co-op store (managed by Mr Hopper, father of Margaret, who married Mac Forrester and who lived in Mount Joy Crescent next door to my parents in their later lives), Crampton's who seemed to maintain a fine display of fruit and veg, even during the war, and then Mr and Mrs Johnson at the busy Elvet Post Office. Beaty Johnson was keen on her cats and the post office always had a certain odour about it. Like a lot of the city, the roadway was composed of grey granite setts, making a bicycle ride quite a bone-shaking experience and in the winter snows the bank could prove too much for some vehicles and traffic chaos would be the result.

* * *

In the Forties there were three shops in Church Street and four in Hallgarth Street. Children's favourite in Church Street was Dobbin's, on the end of Anchorage Terrace, next to St Oswald's Church. Mrs Dobbin sold sweets and despite wartime rationing managed to keep her business going. Birtles, near the Institute, was a small grocer's with a corner door. As you entered a bell summoned Mr Fred Birtles, himself, in a brown overall to serve you. I have only the dimmest memory

of Brown's, which was situated near an arch which led into the old Oswald Court but I think it was a confectioner's. Woodcock's, another grocer's, was at the foot of Hallgarth Street.

Then came Speight's the butcher's, next to an arch which led up to Palmer's Garth. At No 17, on the corner of Mavin Street, was, a general store Miss Dixon's (later Young's, where I lived for several years and now, who would believe it, an Italian restaurant). And at the Mount Joy end was Elliott's, a small general store. As well as being an eager customer in my childhood, I had a personal connection with Mrs Dobbin, through her nephew, Tom Dobbin, of West Cornforth, who was Chief Reporter at the Advertiser when I began work there in 1953. I made quite a poor start and it was thanks to Tom that I survived my six-month probationary period and went on to be passably competent.

BELOW: Dobbins shop, at the end of Anchorage Terrace, an old fashioned sweet shop, opposite St Oswald's school, a children's favourite for many years.

ABOVE: Mostly Elvet lads, this line-up is the Three Hearts of Gold, Church Street, darts club supper, taken on January 26th, 1951. Names as remembered by Mrs Peggy Davies, ex-landlady, who lent the picture are: back (from left), Ronnie Farthing, Nicky Greaves, Dennis Moir, Fred Hall, Fred Ward, Ernie Benson, Matt Lawton, Bill Shotton, Joe Peat; middle row, Harry Plimmer, Ken Livingstone, Jimmy Oliver, Neville Boyd, Andy Davison, Archie Lawton, Billy Walker, Jim Davies (landlord), Jack Rowell; front, Jack Harrison, Nancy Wood, Jean Moir, Peggy Davies (landlady), Hazel Davies, Harry Stevenson and Bily Todd.

The attractively-named Three Hearts of Gold was a popular pub in Church Street and was said by former landlady Peggy Davies to be a former coaching house. Mrs Davies (92? at the time of writing) and her husband Jim ran it from 1937 to the early Fifties. It had once been owned by Joseph Johnson (Durham) Ltd, the brewers, of Elvet, but when that business closed it was taken over by the Westoe Brewery, of South Shields, also then owners of the New Inn.

Now a widow living in The Hallgarth on a development that was once the site of Hallgarth Farm, Mrs Davies recalled that she ran the business almost single-handedly during the war as husband Jim was engaged in war work. He was also a St Oswald's chorister and was, on and off, acting churchwarden over a period of about thirty years.

The pub was conveniently situated virtually opposite the vestry and for some of the men of the church, including the Vicar, the Rev Hilary Morse, it was often the first port of call after Sunday evensong. Mrs Davies brought up two children at the pub, Hazel, who sadly predeceased her, and a son, also named Jim, who was active as a lad in scouting circles. The pub was demolished to make way for the Oswald Court bungalows development.

Chapter IX

HE MIGHT LIVE TILL HE'S 40!

My discharge from Earl's House in 1942 was not the end of the medical profession's interest in my well-being. Now it was deemed I should go to Sherburn Hospital for six-monthly check-ups. Sherburn Hospital began in the 12th century as a leper hospital and down the years adapted its service to the community to the needs of the day, its very isolation being one means of checking the spread of diseases. Monitoring TB was now part of its role but I don't know who paid for keeping a weather eye on my progress as this was before the days of the National Health Service.

The United bus for West Hartlepool, via Sherburn House, ran only every two hours so the routine was to catch the 8.45am service from the New Inn for the journey lasting five or ten minutes. Patients assembled in quite a large room in the dispensary across the road from the entrance to Sherburn House's main complex. It was an austere but highly polished environment and you waited in a sort of reverential silence until it was your turn. Stripped to the waist you were weighed, x-rayed, examined by the doctor – and in my case invariably told to come back in six months.

My imagination might be playing a trick but I have it quite firmly lodged in my mind that I overheard my Aunt Olive, who accompanied me on my early visits, ask the doctor about my long-term prospects. In reply, he said that I might live until I was 40, or words to that effect. What a relief. For a child of only seven or eight that seemed a not unreasonable life expectancy. No immediate danger!

As at Earl's House, I never felt unwell but as the years rolled by, gaining in understanding, I began to grow anxious and frustrated about this continuing surveillance. I know my parents exhibited a great sense of relief on each occasion I was pronounced "clear" of the dreaded TB. Eventually, I think on the intervention of my stepmother Florrie and in some way in response to my own impatience the visits to Sherburn House came to en end.

ABOVE: Posing on the Town Hall steps for Durham Johnston Grammar School prizegiving c1949. The St Oswald's parish contingent includes Clive Titman, of Highwood Terrace (front row, fourth from right) myself right behind him; Bob Cherry, of Houghall (third row, far left with head cocked and wavy hair), behind him Alan Shea, Highwood View; Roger Lightfoot, of Mount Joy Crecent (third row, to the left of the lad with glases), Kenneth Hayton, of Church Street Head (third row, second from right).

I would have been 11 then in 1947; my mother had been gone five years; and I was about to start a new era at Johnston Grammar School. Was it not time to be given the last all-clear? After all, I was living life to the full for a boy of that age without any apparent ill effects.

The experts concurred and we were happily back on the bus home in time for dinner. A lengthy but, no doubt, necessary ordeal had come to an end, and there was an enormous sense of elation. My mother had died of TB. Luckily I escaped its terrible clutches but it was something that haunted my conscious childhood for a good five years or more.

Looking back, the euphoria of that occasion reminds me of even younger days when, as carefee small children in sunny blustery springtime, we ran backwards and forwards across the top of Mount Joy Hill with coats held open, hoping to catch the the breeze and fly away. Oh, and by the way, I carried on with a clean bill of health, through my school-days and beyond to National Service with the Royal Air Force in Singapore. And you will have noted that I made it well past the prophesied 40!

Now see if you can pass the Scholarship. Edward Almond did . . .

County Council of Durham.

EDUCATION DEPARTMENT.

ADMISSION OF
PUPILS TO GRAMMAR SCHOOLS, 1951.

ARITHMETIC (Total Marks 100).

TUESDAY, 30th JANUARY, 1951.

9.30 a.m. to 10.15 a.m.

Write your EXAMINATION NUMBER (not your name) and the name of your school at the top right hand corner of every sheet of paper used.

You may attempt all seven questions and answer them in any order.

Place the number of the question in the margin and leave a space after each answer.

No scrap paper may be used, To obtain full marks you must show all your working on your answer paper.

1. (a) Find the sum of the following numbers – 87, 364, 1428, 79   (5 marks)

   (b) Multiply 284 by 7   (5 marks)

   (c) How many half-pints are there in three gallons?   (5 marks)

   (d) Find the value of $^1/_3 + ^5/_6$ (5 marks)

   (e) How much heavier is a man of 13 st. 3lbs than a boy of 6 stones 5lbs?   (5 marks)

2. Amongst an audience of 3,000 people were 1,897men, 390 women and 257 boys; how many girls were there?   (10 marks)

3. What sum must be added to £37 19s, 11d. to equal 10,000 pence?   (10 marks)

4. How many pieces of cloth each 5yds. 2ft. long can be cut from a roll of length 84 yds. and how much is left over?   (10 marks)

5. Two men set off from the same spot at 10 a.m. and walk in exactly opposite directions, one man going at the rate of 4 miles an hour and the other man at the rate of $3^1/_2$ miles an hour. How far apart will they be at 2.10 p.m.? (Answer in miles and furlongs)   (15 marks)

6. At an entertainment where the price of admission was one shilling a number of people paid 6d. extra for reserved seats. The total amount taken was £10 8s. 6d. and 185 persons were present. How many were in the reserved seats?   (15 marks)

7. A garden is 27 yds. long and 25 yds. wide. Another garden has exactly the same area but is only 15 yds. wide. What is its length?
   Each garden is surrounded by a wire fence with three lines of wire. Assuming there is no overlap or wastage of wire, what is the difference in the lengths of wire required for fencing the two gardens?   (15 marks)

County Council of Durham.

EDUCATION DEPARTMENT.

ADMISSION OF
PUPILS TO GRAMMAR SCHOOLS, 1951.

ENGLISH (Total Marks 100).

TUESDAY, 30th JANUARY, 1951.

10.45 a.m. to 11.30 a.m.

Write your EXAMINATION NUMBER (not your name) and the name of your school at the top right hand corner of every sheet of paper used.

All the four questions may be attempted.

Marks will be deducted for faulty spelling and faulty punctuation.

1. Answer each of the following questions and *be sure that each answer is a COMPLETE SENTENCE.*
   (a) Where are you now?
   (b) What are you doing?
   (c) At what time did you have breakfast?
   (d) How tall are you?
   (e) What colour are your eyes?   (15 marks)

2. Write these sentences as though the event happened yesterday. Begin each answer "Yesterday..."
   (a) The dog runs swiftly.
   (b) Mother sweeps the floor.
   (c) The maid skims the milk.
   (d) Father listens to the radio.
   (e) Uncle is happy at supper time.   (20 marks)

3. Give the authors and titles of poems about FIVE of the following (a different poem for each).

Arrange your answer like this:–

Subject.	Author.	Title.
Ordinary people.	Robert Burns.	The Cottar's Saturday Night.

Flowers, Winter, An incident in History, Birds, Autumn, A fairy tale, An animal, The sea, Sunset, A shepherd, The countryside, Spring, A boy, A river, A famous person, A humorous event, Summer, A girl, Sunrise, A baby.

Write Four lines of ONE of the poems you have named.   (25 marks)

4. Read the following extract and then answer the questions below :–

When darkness fell over the river an ear-splitting orchestra struck up on the bank. Toads and frogs, crickets and mosquitoes croaked or chirped or hummed in a prolonged chorus of many voices. Now and again the shrill scream of a wild cat rang through the darkness, and soon another, and yet another, from birds scared into flight by the night prowlers of the jungle. Once or twice we saw the gleam of a fire in a native hut, and heard bawling voices and the barking of dogs as we slid past in the night. But for the most part we sat alone with the jungle orchestra under the stars, till drowsiness and rain drove us into the cabin of leaves, where we went to sleep with our pistols loose in their holsters.

1. What is an orchestra   (3 marks)

2. What was the jungle orchestra?   (3 marks)

3. Which creatures croaked?   (2 marks)
   Which creatures chirped?   (2 marks)
   Which creatures hummed?   (2 marks)

4. Explain the following :–
   Prowlers.   (2 marks)
   Drowsiness   (2 marks)
   Ear-splitting   (3 marks)
   Holsters   (3 marks)
   Prolonged chorus   (3 marks)
   Scared into flight   (3 marks)

5. What phrase suggests that these persons were in a boat on the river?   (3 marks)

6. Select words or phrases which describe loud noise.   (3 marks)

7. What protection had they against the weather?   (3 marks)

8. Why were the pistols left loose in their holsters?   (3 marks)

                                                                    (40 marks)

Acknowledgements

I AM grateful to Win Colman (née Winifred Slater), Peggy Davies, Dorothy Summerbell (Shea), Mary Almond, Jennifer Blair (Coates) Brian Shaw and Mrs Heather Eaton, head teacher at St Oswald's School, for the loan of pictures and helpful information.

ALSO to Durham City Reference Library and Durham County Record Office; and to Paul Marsh and Matthew Usher, of the *Lynn News* photographic department, for copying contributed pictures

SPECIAL ACKNOWLEDGEMENT to Win Colman for her enthusiastic support and liaison with Durham St Oswald's Church members and potential contributors.

The author welcomes comments, clarifications and corrections arising from this work.
Write to: David Young, The Shieling, 19 Orchard Grove, West Winch, King's Lynn, Norfolk PE33 0JZ. (01553 840253)